THE DARK SIDE OF SOCIAL MEDIA

THE DARK SIDE OF SOCIAL MEDIA

Psychological, Managerial, and Societal Perspectives

PAVICA SHELDON
*Communications Arts Department, The University of Alabama in Huntsville,
Huntsville, AL, United States*

PHILIPP A. RAUSCHNABEL
*Fakultät für Betriebswirtschaft (College of Business),
Universität der Bundeswehr München, Neubiberg, Germany*

JAMES M. HONEYCUTT
*Organizational Behavior, Coaching, and Consulting,
Naveen Jindal School of Management, The University of Texas at Dallas,
Richardson, TX, United States*

ACADEMIC PRESS
An imprint of Elsevier

Academic Press is an imprint of Elsevier
125 London Wall, London EC2Y 5AS, United Kingdom
525 B Street, Suite 1650, San Diego, CA 92101, United States
50 Hampshire Street, 5th Floor, Cambridge, MA 02139, United States
The Boulevard, Langford Lane, Kidlington, Oxford OX5 1GB, United Kingdom

Notices
Knowledge and best practice in this field are constantly changing. As new research and experience
broaden our understanding, changes in research methods, professional practices, or medical
treatment may become necessary.

Practitioners and researchers must always rely on their own experience and knowledge in
evaluating and using any information, methods, compounds, or experiments described herein. In
using such information or methods they should be mindful of their own safety and the safety of
others, including parties for whom they have a professional responsibility.

To the fullest extent of the law, neither the Publisher nor the authors, contributors, or editors,
assume any liability for any injury and/or damage to persons or property as a matter of products
liability, negligence or otherwise, or from any use or operation of any methods, products,
instructions, or ideas contained in the material herein.

British Library Cataloguing-in-Publication Data
A catalogue record for this book is available from the British Library

Library of Congress Cataloging-in-Publication Data
A catalog record for this book is available from the Library of Congress

ISBN: 978-0-12-815917-0

For Information on all Academic Press publications
visit our website at https://www.elsevier.com/books-and-journals

Publisher: Nikki Levy
Acquisition Editor: Joslyn Chaiprasert-Paguio
Editorial Project Manager: Barbara Makinster
Production Project Manager: Paul Prasad Chandramohan
Cover Designer: Mathew Limbert

Typeset by MPS Limited, Chennai, India

Working together
to grow libraries in
developing countries

www.elsevier.com • www.bookaid.org

Dedication

I dedicate this book to those who are not addicted to social media. It is sad that social media addiction does not enhance cultural creativity and imagination—as opposed to simply playing entertainment games, which do not contribute to society. We need to move onward and upward, as I say.

James M. Honeycutt

I dedicate this book to my wife and daughter!

Philipp A. Rauschnabel

Contents

Section I

THE DARK SIDE OF PERSONAL SOCIAL MEDIA USE

Section II

THE DARK SIDE OF PROFESSIONAL SOCIAL MEDIA USE

Section III

THE DARK SIDE OF SOCIAL MEDIA USE FOR SOCIETIES

Preface

Social media influence the way we live our lives and conduct business. Scholars have discussed the use of social media to build personal and professional relationships, but little attention has been given to the negative aspects of social media. The purpose of this book is to complement the numerous empirical findings on the "bright" side of social media with a less bright perspective. *The Dark Side of Social Media* involves understanding what research has told us about social media influence on our personal, professional, and public lives and practices. This book is intended for scholars, college students, social media professionals, and members of the general public interested in the social sciences—including media psychology and addiction, interpersonal relationships, consumer behavior, journalism trends, and organizational communication. The book has additional applications in social work, educational psychology, and sociology.

Chapter 1, Social Media and Mental and Physical Health, examines the relationship between social media and mental and physical health. It discusses topics such as stress, depression, sleeping disorders, and addiction. Chapter 2, Narcissism as a Predictor of Self-Presentation, focuses on narcissism, generational differences in narcissism, intercultural distinctions, and types of narcissists using social media platforms such as Facebook and Instagram. Narcissism is a popular topic with the advent of cultural technology and instantaneous gratification through media access. In Chapter 3, Cyberstalking and Bullying, we discuss cyberstalking and cyberbullying, especially among children and college students. Cyberbullying is prevalent given the ability to protect self-identity with the use of different personas and media identities. Chapter 4, Negative Social Comparisons on Social Network Sites, looks at different types of comparisons people engage in because of social media. Chapter 5, Social Media and Relationship Drama, explores the "dark side" further, looking at problems that social media cause in both romantic and friendship relationships. Chapter 6, Social Media Monitoring: A Cautionary View, focuses on the risks of social media marketing for organizations and their reputation—in particular a new form of communication crises, so-called collaborative brand attacks or online firestorms. In Chapter 7, Online Firestorms: Collaborative Brand Attacks, we look at social media monitoring and discuss the numerous challenges and limitations that professionals have to deal with, such as extreme user opinions, social media bots, satire, closed channels, and intransparent tools. Chapter 8, Social Media Privacy, focuses on how we manage privacy online, privacy paradox, and also provides recommendations for parents and teachers to make sure that children are safe when using social media. The final chapter, that is, Chapter 9, Social Media Lies and Rumors, explores lies and rumors that occur on social media. It includes a background on deception, as well as how rumors are spread on social media.

Acknowledgments

In terms of acknowledgments, I appreciate Pavica asking me to contribute to this book as a coauthor. I was her major professor, and now she is chair of the communications department at the University of Alabama in Huntsville. She continues my legacy.

James M. Honeycutt

I would like to acknowledge all of the students at the University of Alabama in Huntsville who have helped with this book, especially Latoya Tisdale Binford and Brittney Sykes.

Pavica Sheldon

I thank my co-authors Nadine Kammerlander and Björn S. Ivens for the great collaboration on our paper on social media firestorms (Rauschnabel, P. A., Kammerlander, N., & Ivens, B. S. (2016). Collaborative brand attacks in social media: Exploring the antecedents, characteristics, and consequences of a new form of brand crises. Journal of Marketing Theory and Practice, 24(4), 381–410) which is the basis for chapter 7 in this book.

Philipp A. Rauschnabel

THE DARK SIDE OF PERSONAL SOCIAL MEDIA USE

CHAPTER

1

Social Media and Mental and Physical Health

OUTLINE

STRESS AND ANXIETY

Stress is defined as a group or events consisting of a stimulus (i.e., a stressor), which triggers a reaction in a person's brain about whether or not there are resources necessary to meet the demands placed on them by the stimulus, which then sparks a physiological fight-or-flight response (Campisi et al., 2012; Nabi, Prestin, & So, 2013). Researchers (Stevens, Humphrey, Wheatley, & Galliher, 2011) have found that stress relief is one reason undergraduate students used Facebook. Number of Facebook friends was associated with greater perceived social support, which then was associated with reduced stress, and, in turn, reduced physical illness and greater psychological well-being (Stevens et al., 2011). Other studies (e.g., Duggan, Heath, Lewis, & Baxter, 2012) have also found that social support offered through social networking sites (SNSs) includes increased emotional support, self-disclosure, reduced social anxiety, and belongingness.

Depending on the situation, however, social media can also cause stress. For example, Bevan, Gomez, and Sparks' (2014) survey of adult Facebook users aged 18−70 revealed that the more time spent on and the more social network memberships, the higher stress and the lower quality of life. In addition, users who shared important, bad health news on Facebook had higher stress and lower quality of life than users who did not. Chen and Lee (2013) also found that more frequent Facebook interaction is associated with greater psychological distress. Time and energy needed to manage multiple SNSs might be especially taxing. Updating and maintaining a variety of online identities take time.

Anxiety disorders are the second leading cause of disability among all psychiatric disorders. Most anxiety disorders peak amid emerging and early adulthood (Whiteford et al., 2013). In Campisi et al. (2012) study comprising mostly female (88%) US undergraduates, nearly half participants reported delaying responses to Facebook friend requests due to anxiety about the request. In addition, the social network size was significantly related to the rate of upper respiratory infections (URI), such that, the larger the social network, the greater the incidence rate of URI. Almost a third of respondents stated that being defriended made them angry or sad.

Vannucci, Flannery, and Ohannessian (2017) also examined the impact of time spent using social media on anxiety symptoms and severity in emerging adults. Their results revealed that more time spent using social media was significantly associated with greater symptoms of dispositional anxiety. Labrague (2014) looked at Facebook use as influence on depression, stress, and anxiety among college students in Philippines. The results of a study revealed a positive correlation between the amount of time spent on Facebook and anxiety and depression scores. Labrague (2014) argued that this may be due to the fact that investing so much time on Facebook may increase the possibility of encountering negative comments, explicit news, and negative updates from Facebook friends, which may trigger the developments of these emotional states. It may also limit socializing time. Other reasons include negative feedback or cyberbullying from peers (Vannucci et al., 2017), as well as negative social comparisons.

DEPRESSION

Depression is an affective disorder characterized by (1) a depressive mood, (2) loss of interest and joy, and (3) elevated tiredness, reduced motivation, and activity that affect human cognition (Dilling, Mombour, & Schmidt, 2011). Depressed individuals hold negative views of themselves and their world (Beck, 1987). It is predicted that depression will become the leading cause of disability in high-income countries by 2030 (Mathers & Loncar, 2006).

While some studies (e.g., Valenzuela, Park, & Kee, 2009) have found that time spent in online communication can reduce depressive symptoms through online social support and social connectedness, social media use has been associated with the development of depression (Primack, Swanier, Georgiopoulos, Land, & Fine, 2009). Most studies have found that the amount of social media use is less important than *how* social media are used (Lin et al., 2016; Seabrook, Kern, & Rickard, 2016; Shensa et al., 2017; Twenge, Joiner, Rogers, & Martin, 2017). For example, Lup, Trub, and Rosenthal (2015) found that more passive forms of use (e.g., browsing others' profiles without posting own material) contribute to a depressed mood. Passively looking at others' photo of vacations or social events we were not invited to trigger resentment, envy, and loneliness (Krasnova, Wenninger, Widjaja, & Buxmann, 2013). Having strangers as friends on social media also contributes to greater depressive symptoms (Lup et al., 2015). While we know how our friends and acquaintances live, we are more likely to exhibit attribution error toward people we do not know (Chou & Edge, 2012).

Adolescents score high on depression (Wang et al., 2018). Frison and Eggermont's (2017) self-report data from 671 Flemish adolescent revealed that Instagram browsing at Time 1 was related to increases in adolescents' depressed mood at Time 2. Furthermore, Primack et al.'s (2017) survey of 1787 American young adults uncovered that participants who used 7–11 social media platforms had substantially higher odds of having increased levels of both depression and anxiety symptoms compared to adolescents who used 0–2 social media platforms.

Wang et al. (2018) studied Chinese high school students to examine the relationship between their social media use, depression, and rumination. Rumination is defined as repetitive thoughts and behaviors on symptoms, causes, and consequences of past personal distress (Nolen-Hoeksema, 2000). A longitudinal research has revealed that rumination predicts the onset of depression (Wilkinson, Croudace, & Goodyer, 2013). Certain features of SNSs could facilitate rumination, such as status updates and passive use (Shaw, Timpano, Tran, & Joormann, 2015), especially among adolescents with a low self-esteem (Wang et al., 2018). Rumination might include thoughts such as "I should have never posted that" or "I wished this person did not say that on my wall."

Frison and Eggermont's (2016) survey of European high schoolers also revealed a positive association between passive Facebook use and adolescent girls' depressed mood. This negative impact of passive Facebook use on adolescents' well-being was explained by social comparison theory (Festinger, 1954). According to social comparison theory, we either compare to those who are like us or better than us. Upward comparison is comparison to others we perceive to be socially better than ourselves, which often causes negative effect. In some cases, especially when online feedback is not available (e.g., nobody comments on one's status update or new photo album), active Facebook use can also lead to depression (Deters & Mehl, 2013). Chapter 4, Negative Social Comparisons on Social Network Sites, discusses the theory and comparisons that happen through social media.

SUICIDE RATES

Within the last 20 years, suicide rates among adolescents and young adults have drastically increased. Due to social media–induced depression, suicides rates have increased in the United States. In two nationally representative surveys of US adolescents in grades 8 through 12 and national statistics on suicide deaths for those ages 13–18, adolescents' depressive symptoms, suicide-related outcomes, and suicide rates increased between 2010 and 2015, especially among females (Twenge et al., 2017). This can happen for a variety of reasons. First, social media can facilitate finding detailed information on suicide methods. In Twenge et al. (2017) study, 8% of teens who spent 5 hours per day on an electronic device had at least one suicide risk factor, compared to 33% of teens who spent 2 hours a day on an electronic device.

Ueda, Mori, Matsubayashi, and Sawada (2017) found that suicides by relatively young entertainers generated a large number of posts on Twitter and were followed by an increase in population suicides. In contrast, no discernible increase in suicide counts was observed when Twitter users did not show much interest in prominent suicidal deaths. Their study collected over 1 million individual messages (tweets) posted on Twitter, which were related to 26 prominent figures in Japan who died by suicide between 2010 and 2014. The rise in suicide rates was explained by a copycat behavior, or the "Werther effect." The "Werther effect" phenomenon is one of the main sources of negative externalities of suicide (Ueda, Mori, & Matsubayashi, 2014). In addition, social learning theory might explain the observed change in suicide rates after media coverage of prominent suicides (Pirkis & Blood, 2010). The theory implies that media can make suicides appear acceptable, especially when modeled by someone's celebrity status.

SLEEPING PATTERNS

College students often report a lack of sleep—in quality and duration. This can have effects on everyday life, including poor academic performance, confusion, reduced intellectual capacity, and altered motor function. Studies examining the impact of social media on sleep revealed negative effects, especially among adolescents.

Burke (2016) argued that technology impacts sleep quality in three main ways: through light emission, content, and timing. Light emission affects our circadian rhythm. The bright light emitted from an electronic device reinforces the message to the brain to stay awake. Individuals who frequently checked social media throughout the day had increased risk of having sleep problems (Burke, 2016). In addition, engaging with exciting information before bed triggers emotional and hormonal responses that can reduce the ability to fall and stay asleep (Levenson, Shensa, Sidani, Colditz, & Primack, 2016). Whipps, Byra, Gerow, and Guseman (2018) conducted a study to determine the association between presence and use of media devices at nighttime, such as tablets and smart phones, and sleep patterns of first-semester college students. Results revealed that first-year students reported chronically low levels of sleep compared to the American Academy of Sleep Medicine and Sleep Research Society recommendation of 7 or more hours of sleep per night (Watson et al., 2015). Nighttime media usage negatively affects sleep quality. Participants who more frequently reported using social media or texting after bed were more likely to report sleep interruptions by their devices (Whipps et al., 2018). Media use close to or after bedtime results in delayed bedtime, longer time to fall asleep, and reduced sleep time (Cain & Gradisar, 2010).

Smahel, Wright, and Černíková (2015) focused on children's perceptions of the negative health-related consequences linked to their technology use. They collected data from children in nine European countries. Results of a study revealed the support for the displacement hypothesis (Endestad, Heim, Kaare, Torgersen, & Bae Brandtzæg, 2011) that the more time spent with media, the less time children devoted to other activities. These children often reported poor health, experiencing a variety of eye problems, eating problems, headaches, and tiredness. In some cases, children experience those problems after 30 minutes of technology use. They also experienced mental health problems, including their head, aggressive behaviors, and sleeping problems, including nightmares (Smahel et al., 2015).

FITNESS, HEALTH, AND EATING HABITS

Most recently, studies examined the association between social media use and healthy eating in college-aged population. Sidani, Shensa, Hoffman, Hanmer, and Primack's (2016) study with 1745 participants aged 19–32 revealed a strong association between social media use and eating concerns. Individuals with high social media use were at risk for developing eating disorders. This is not surprising considering that most social media platforms place strong emphasis on visuals.

Syed-Abdul et al. (2013) investigated anorexia-related information disseminated through YouTube videos. Three doctors reviewed 140 videos and classified them as informative, pro-anorexia, and others. Their results revealed that pro-anorexia content is highly favored rated by its viewers, more than informative videos. Moreno et al.'s (2013) study with college students also revealed that college students who used the Internet primarily for social networking had lower levels of vigorous physical activity. Overuse of social media can also cause fatigue and eye problems. It can also harm relationships. The problematic overuse of social media is also known as a social media addiction.

ADDICTION TO SOCIAL MEDIA

Social media addiction is a subset of Internet addiction dealing specifically with SNSs (Longstreet & Brooks, 2017). With the widespread adoption of social network sites such as Instagram, Facebook, and Snapchat, this problem has become more prominent. Previous research (e.g., Limayem & Cheung, 2011) has found that enjoyment elicited through using social media can stimulate the development of a strong use habit, which, in turn, causes high levels of addiction (Turel & Serenko, 2012).

Although not officially classified as a disorder in Diagnostic and Statistical Manual of Mental Disorders-5, technology addiction is related to a number of mental health problems (Savci & Aysan, 2017), including depression (e.g., Brunborg, Mentzoni, & Frøyland, 2014; Demirci, Akgönül, & Akpinar, 2015), impulsivity (e.g., Billieux, Van Der Linden, D'Acremont, Ceschi, & Zermatten, 2007), sleep quality (e.g., Demirci et al., 2015; Woods & Scott, 2016), well-being (e.g., Demirci et al., 2015), self-esteem (Bozoglan, Demirer, & Sahin, 2013; van Rooij, Schoenmakers, van den Eijnden, Vermulst, & van de Mheen, 2012), and academic performance (Brunborg et al., 2014).

Rosen, Cheever, and Carrier (2012) coined the term "iDisorder," to explain the negative relationship between technology use and psychological health. iDisorder includes changes in your brain's ability to process information and relate to world due to our daily use of media and technology. Mazer and Ledbetter's (2012) study revealed that compulsive Internet usage predicted physical symptoms, such as headaches, stomachaches, and eye problems.

A recent meta-analysis determined that approximately 6% of the world's populations have at least a base level of Internet addiction (Cheng & Li, 2014). According to He, Turel, and Bechara (2017), the addiction to social media includes the following symptoms: salience (preoccupation with the behavior), mood change (performing the behavior to relieve or reduce aversive emotional states), tolerance (increasing engagement in the behavior over time to attain initial mood modifying effects), withdrawal symptoms (negative feelings and discomfort when the behavior is reduced or prohibited), conflict (putting off other activities as well as one's own and others' needs because of the behavior), and relapse (unsuccessfully trying to cut down or control the behavior).

Causes of addiction. In order to understand consequences of social media addiction, one has to understand what is causing it. Past studies have found that a combination of social, psychological, and biological factors, as well as the content of social media sites stimulate addiction (e.g., Griffiths, 2005; Hormes, Kearns, & Alix Timko, 2014). For some people, social media is a way to escape from reality and stresses of daily lives (Sheldon & Bryant, 2016).

A number of studies have looked at how personality traits and states can predict social media addiction. Sheldon and Sykes (2018) examined whether life-position indicators and personality traits were significant predictors of Facebook, Instagram, and Snapchat addictions. Their analysis revealed that social activity was a significant predictor of variance in Instagram addiction scores (6.3%). Those addicted to Instagram are more socially active. This makes sense as most people use Instagram for documentation purposes (Sheldon & Bryant, 2016). Individuals who travel and attend events (are "socially active") often take many pictures to document their memories. As a visual social network, Instagram is an ideal forum for it.

Sheldon and Sykes (2018) also found that the fear of missing out (FOMO) was a significant predictor of social media addiction with respect to Facebook, Instagram, and Snapchat use. It explained the most variance in addiction scores for Snapchat (20.5%). It also explained a sizeable amount of variance in scores for Facebook addiction (16.6%) and Instagram addiction (12.6%). Conlin, Billings, and Averset (2016) suggest that under the self-determination theory (SDT), controlled motivation results in FOMO, in that individuals feel pressure to fit in with a large social group and may fear that they are missing out when they are not part of a cultural conversation about media. They also argue that SDT's proposed need for relatedness may be the most relevant to FOMO, as fear of missing out on experiences and social connections can cause people "to make decisions based on timing more than personal desires" (Conlin et al., 2016).

Blackwell, Leaman, Tramposch, Osborne, and Liss (2017) did a study to investigate whether extraversion, neuroticism, attachment style, and FOMO were predictors of social media use and addiction. FOMO is fear that other people are having fun without you (Przybylski, Murayama, DeHaan, & Gladwell, 2013). While neuroticism and FOMO predicted social media use, only FOMO predicted social media addiction. In another study (Wilson, Fornasier, & White, 2010), extraversion was a predictor of social media use and addiction. While it seems natural for extraverts to use social media more because they crave social interaction, addiction might be less influential as they interact with others face to face as well

(Blackwell et al., 2017). Beyens, Frison, and Eggermont (2016) also examined the FOMO relationship to social media use and addiction among adolescents. They found that a strong need to belong, and need for popularity leads to increased Facebook use and also increased FOMO. FOMO was associated with increased stress related to Facebook use. Beyens et al. (2016) argued that constant access to social media further feeds adolescents' FOMO. As a result, studies have found that teens may lose sleep because they feel a constant need to use media, reportedly keeping their mobile phones by the bed and under their pillows in order to avoid missing messages at night (Lenhart, Ling, Campbell, & Purcell, 2010).

Brailovskaia and Margraf (2017) studied Facebook addiction disorder (FAD) in a German student sample over a period of 1 year. They found that FAD was significantly related to the narcissistic personality trait and to negative mental health variables (depression, anxiety, and stress symptoms). Narcissists may prefer Facebook as it allows them to connect with a large audience. They spend more time thinking about Facebook than others, planning their online self-presentation (Brailovskaia & Margraf, 2017).

For people with low self-esteem, social media has become a safe haven to interact. Andreassen, Pallesen, and Griffiths (2017) examined addictive social media use in over 23,500 Norwegians ($M_{age} = 35.8$ years) and found addiction to be related to lower self-esteem and higher narcissism score. Social media applications are ideal social arenas for individuals who are attracted to ego-enhancing activities (Wang, Jackson, Zhang, & Su, 2012) as those platforms may fulfill their need for affiliation and confirm the sense of an idealized self. Andreassen et al. (2017) found higher social media addiction score among young, female, and single. For single people, social media such as Tinder represent ground for meeting potential partners (Andreassen et al., 2017).

Durkee et al. (2012) investigated the prevalence of pathological Internet use (PIU) and maladaptive Internet use (MIU) among adolescents in 11 European countries. They found a prevalence of PIU among 4.4% adolescents, especially those lacking familiar support. Adolescents living without a biological parent, low parental involvement, and parental unemployment were the most influential factors in determining MIU and PIU.

Hong, Huang, Lin, and Chiu (2014) found that depressed university students tend to be addicted to Facebook. They defined this addiction as FAD, which refers to an individual's inability to control one's own actions on Facebook. In their study the more time students spent on Facebook, the higher was their addiction score. Individuals not in relationships are also more likely to develop addiction to technology (Kuss, Griffiths, Karila, & Billieux, 2014).

Biological explanation for addiction includes insufficient amount of serotonin and dopamine (Beard, 2005). While serotonin is responsible for maintaining mood balance (Medicinenet.com, 2014), dopamine is a chemical that controls arousal and motivation and is released in the brain as a result of rewarding and pleasurable experiences (e.g., food) (Arias-Carrión & Pöppel, 2007). One of the rewarding experiences that might result in an increase in dopamine is the use of social media to play games, receive "likes" and "favorites" on Instagram photos (Horn, 2012). In fact, when someone likes your Instagram post, it is a very similar experience to taking a drug as far as your brain is concerned.

Preoccupation with the Internet can gratify other addictions (Liu & Potenza, 2007; Schaffer, Hall, & Bilt, 2000). For example, Gilbert, Murphy, and McNally (2011) found a moderate positive correlation between addiction to second life and various compulsions in real life such as shopping, sex, gambling, drug, and alcohol addictions. However, research still has not provided sufficient validity to determine whether Internet addiction is strongly related to other types of addictions.

Consequences of addiction. Addiction to social media can have detrimental outcomes. Studies have recorded declining school performances among college students (Tsitsika et al., 2011), decrease in the quality of interpersonal relationships (Milani, Osualdella, & Di Blasio, 2009), and negative impact on identity formation, which also includes negative comparisons to other (Stefanone, Lackaff, & Rosen, 2011).

Gender differences in addiction have been documented as well. Men are more likely to be addicted to video games and online gambling, while women tend to overuse social media and shop online (Andreassen et al., 2017; Chiu, Hong, & Chiu, 2013; Davenport, Houston, & Griffiths, 2012; Durkee et al., 2012; Ferguson, Coulson, & Barnett, 2011; Kuss et al., 2014). College students around the world experience a similar addiction to social media. When asked to give up mobile phones, the Internet, social media, and television for 24 hours, young adults (ages 17–23) from 10 different countries reported significant mental and physical distress (Moeller, 2010). The study found that addiction to technology was similar to a drug addiction.

DeWeese (2014) surveyed students and teachers at affluent public school in San Francisco Bay area. Many of the teachers interviewed agreed that there is an epidemic of anxiety and depression as well as an addiction to texting. Students were also less connected to their peers because of technology. When asked about multitasking, 90% of students said they use various technologies at the same time. Only 10% said that they do one thing at a time. Many feel the FOMO.

Selfies. Addiction with selfies, especially in youth, affects mental health (Pal, 2015). Selfies are self-portrait photographs, typically taken with a smartphone and shared on various social media sites (Qiu, Lu, Yang, Qu, & Zhu, 2015). The American Psychiatric Association during its annual meeting in Chicago (2014) coined a term "Selfitis," which is defined as the obsessive compulsive desire to take photos of one's self and post them on social media as a way to make up for the lack of self-esteem (Kaur & Vig, 2016). There are three levels of this addiction: (1) "borderline selfitis," which includes taking photos of one's self at least three times per day but not posting them on social media; (2) "acute selfitis," which includes taking photos of one's self at least three times a day and posting each of the photos on social media; (3) "chronic selfitis," which includes uncontrollable urge to take photos of one's self round the clock and posting the photos on social media more than six times every day (AdoboChron, 2014).

> The word "selfie" was selected as the Word of the Year by The Oxford English Dictionary in 2013 (Oxford Dictionaries). However, the origin of selfies dates back to Robert Cornelius, an American pioneer in photography, who produced a daguerreotype of himself in 1839. This was the first photograph of a person. The first use of the word selfie in media appeared in an Australian Internet forum on September 13, 2002 (Kaur & Vig, 2016). Instagram introduced the first hashtag selfie in 2011 (Sung, Lee, Kim, & Choi, 2016).

Deng et al. (2018) explored selfie-posting behavior across Facebook, Twitter, Instagram, and Snapchat and its relationship with psychological well-being. Their results revealed that Snapchat was the platform with the greatest number of selfies posted, followed by Facebook, Twitter, and Instagram (Deng et al., 2018). Posting selfies was also related to loneliness and depression.

Selfies' popularity is on the rise. On average, people report posting nine selfies per week (FramesDirect, 2015), more by females than males (Sorokowski et al., 2015).

SOLUTIONS

SNSs are increasingly affecting mental and physical health of teenagers and young adults. Researchers and practitioners have proposed a number of strategies to combat the problem. Deep (2015) proposed three solutions: (1) education and awareness, (2) engagement in extracurricular activities, and (3) restrictions and limitations. The most important solution according to Deep (2015) is education. Schools can provide parents with education on the harmful effects of social media exposure while also opening up a dialogue between educators and students. Teachers can encourage creative person-to-person interaction between students instead of allowing them to look at computer screens for long hours. Extracurricular activities could also help young people with expressing their creativity outside of social media (Deep, 2015). In extreme cases, restrictions should be placed on teens who overuse the Internet. Burke (2016) suggests parents to establish a sleep hygiene routine that structures a set of guidelines for social media interactions. For example, devices could be turned off an hour or two before an appropriate bedtime, so to reduce negative effect of social media on sleep in adolescents.

CONCLUSION

In conclusion, studies show a negative influence of social media on one's mental and physical health. In general the more time someone spends with social media, the more stressed, anxious or depressed he or she is. This is especially true for adolescent and passive users. Participants who more frequently reported using social media were more likely to report sleep interruptions by their devices. Another problem is social media addiction. Personality traits, FOMO, and stimulating content contribute to social media addiction. Detrimental outcomes include mental distress, decrease in the quality of interpersonal relationships, and declining school or work performance. More research is needed to understand the full scope of social media impact on mental and physical health.

References

AdoboChron. (2014). American psychiatric association makes it official: Selfie a mental disorder. *The Adobo Chronicles*. Retrieved from https://adobochronicles.com/2014/03/31/american-psychiatric-association-makes-it-official-selfie-a-mental-disorder/.

Andreassen, C. S., Pallesen, S., & Griffiths, M. D. (2017). The relationship between addictive use of social media, narcissism, and self-esteem: Findings from a large national

survey. *Addictive Behaviors*, *64*, 287−293. Available from https://doi.org/10.1016/
j.addbeh.2016.03.006.

Arias-Carrión, Ó., & Pöppel, E. (2007). Dopamine, learning, and reward-seeking behavior.
Acta Neurobiologiae Experimentalis, *67*(4), 481−488.

Beard, K. W. (2005). Internet addiction: A review of current assessment techniques and
potential assessment questions. *CyberPsychology & Behavior*, *8*, 7−14. Available from
https://doi.org/10.1089/cpb.2005.8.7.

Beck, A. T. (1987). Cognitive models of depression. *The Journal of Cognitive Psychotherapy:
An International Quarterly*, *1*, 5−37.

Bevan, J. L., Gomez, R., & Sparks, L. (2014). Disclosures about important life events on
Facebook: Relationships with stress and quality of life. *Computers in Human Behavior*,
39246−39253. Available from https://doi.org/10.1016/j.chb.2014.07.021.

Beyens, I., Frison, E., & Eggermont, S. (2016). "I don't want to miss a thing": Adolescents'
fear of missing out and its relationship to adolescents' social needs, Facebook use, and
Facebook related stress. *Computers in Human Behavior*, *64*, 1−8.

Billieux, J., Van Der Linden, M., D'Acremont, M., Ceschi, G., & Zermatten, A. (2007). Does
impulsivity relate to perceived dependence on and actual use of the mobile phone?
Applied Cognitive Psychology, *21*(4), 527−537. Available from https://doi.org/10.1002/
acp.1289.

Blackwell, D., Leaman, C., Tramposch, R., Osborne, C., & Liss, M. (2017). Extraversion,
neuroticism, attachment style and fear of missing out as predictors of social media use
and addiction. *Personality and Individual Differences*, *116*, 69−72.

Bozoglan, B., Demirer, V., & Sahin, I. (2013). Loneliness, self-esteem, and life satisfaction as
predictors of Internet addiction: A cross-sectional study among Turkish university students. *Scandinavian Journal of Psychology*, *54*(4), 313−319. Available from https://doi.
org/10.1111/sjop.12049.

Brailovskaia, J., & Margraf, J. (2017). Facebook addiction disorder (FAD) among German
students—A longitudinal approach. *PLoS One*, *12*(12), 1−15. Available from https://
doi.org/10.1371/journal.pone.0189719.

Brunborg, G. S., Mentzoni, R. A., & Frøyland, L. R. (2014). Is video gaming, or video game
addiction, associated with depression, academic achievement, heavy episodic drinking,
or conduct problems? *Journal of Behavioral Addictions*, *3*(1), 27−32. Available from
https://doi.org/10.1556/JBA.3.2014.002.

Burke, S. M. (2016). The impact of media use on sleep in adolescents. *Journal of
Pediatric Nursing*, *31*(5), 556−558. Available from https://doi.org/10.1016/j.pedn.2016.
06.003.

Cain, N., & Gradisar, M. (2010). Electronic media use and sleep in school-aged children
and adolescents: A review. *Sleep Medicine*, *11*, 735−742.

Campisi, J., Bynog, P., McGehee, H., Oakland, J. C., Quirk, S., Taga, C., & Taylor, M.
(2012). Facebook, stress and incidence of upper respiratory infection in undergraduate
college students. *Cyberpsychology, Behavior, and Social Networking*, *15*, 675−681.
Available from https://doi.org/10.1089/cyber.2012.0156.

Chen, W., & Lee, K. (2013). Sharing, liking, commenting, and distressed? The pathway
between Facebook interaction and psychological distress. *Cyberpsychology, Behavior, &
Social Networking*, *16*, 728−734. Available from https://doi.org/10.1089/cyber.2012.0272.

Cheng, C., & Li, A. Y. (2014). Internet addiction prevalence and quality of real life:
A meta-analysis of 31 nations across seven world regions. *Cyberpsychology, Behavior, &
Social Networking*, *17*, 755−760. Available from https://doi.org/10.1089/cyber.
2014.0317.

Chiu, S.-I., Hong, F.-Y., & Chiu, S.-L. (2013). An analysis on the correlation and gender difference between college students' Internet addiction and mobile phone addiction in

Taiwan. *ISRN Addiction, 2013*, 360607. Available from https://doi.org/10.1155/2013/360607.

Chou, H. G., & Edge, N. (2012). 'They are happier and having better lives than I am': The impact of using Facebook on perceptions of others' lives. *Cyberpsychology, Behavior & Social Networking, 15*(2), 117−121. Available from https://doi.org/10.1089/cyber.2011.0324.

Conlin, L., Billings, A. C., & Averset, L. (2016). Time-shifting vs. appointment viewing: The role of fear of missing out within TV consumption behaviors. *Communication & Society, 29*(4), 151−164. Available from https://doi.org/10.15581/003.29.4.151-164.

Davenport, K., Houston, J. E., & Griffiths, M. D. (2012). Excessive eating and compulsive buying behaviors in women: An empirical pilot study examining reward sensitivity, anxiety, impulsivity, self-esteem and social desirability. *International Journal of Mental Health and Addiction, 10*, 474−489. Available from https://doi.org/10.1007/s11469-011-9332-7.

Deep, G. (2015). Social media and the mental health of teenagers: An insight. *Indian Journal of Health & Wellbeing, 6*(7), 741−743.

Demirci, K., Akgönül, M., & Akpinar, A. (2015). Relationship of smartphone use severity with sleep quality, depression, and anxiety in university students. *Journal of Behavioral Addictions, 4*(2), 85-−892. Available from https://doi.org/10.1556/2006.4.2015.010.

Deng, T., Ma, M., Zhao, X., JuYoung, O., Syed, L., Saleem, A. H., & Alhabash, E. (2018). Psychological well-being and selfie posting on social media: Does posting selfie make you better or worse. In: *Paper presented at the International Communication Association conference*. Prague, Czech Republic.

Deters, F. G., & Mehl, M. R. (2013). Does posting Facebook status updates increase or decrease loneliness? An online social networking experiment. *Social Psychological and Personality Science, 4*, 1−8. Available from https://doi.org/10.1177/1948550612469233.

DeWeese, K. L. (2014). *Screen time, how much is too much? The social and emotional costs of technology on the adolescent brain* (Master's thesis). Dominican University of California.

Dilling, H., Mombour, W., & Schmidt, M. H. (2011). *Internationale Klassifikation psychischer Störungen [International classification of mental disorders]* (eighth ed.). Bern: Huber.

Duggan, J. M., Heath, N. L., Lewis, S. P., & Baxter, A. L. (2012). An examination of the scope and nature of non-suicidal self-injury online activities: Implications for school mental health professionals. *School Mental Health, 4*(1), 56−67. Available from https://doi.org/10.1007/s12310-011-9065-6.

Durkee, T., Kaess, M., Carli, V., Parzer, P., Wasserman, C., Floderus, B., ... Wasserman, D. (2012). Prevalence of pathological internet use among adolescents in Europe: Demographic and social factors. *Addiction, 107*, 2210−2222. Available from https://doi.org/10.1111/j.1360-0443.2012.03946.x.

Endestad, T., Heim, J., Kaare, B., Torgersen, L., & Bae Brandtzæg, P. (2011). Media user types among young children and social displacement. *NORDICOM Review, 32*(1), 17−30.

Ferguson, C. J., Coulson, M., & Barnett, J. (2011). A meta-analysis of pathological gaming prevalence and comorbidity with mental health, academic and social problems. *Journal of Psychiatric Research, 45*, 1573−1578. Available from https://doi.org/10.1016/j.jpsychires.2011.09.005.

Festinger, L. (1954). A theory of social comparison processes. *Human Relations, 7*, 117−140. Available from https://doi.org/10.1177/001872675400700202.

FramesDirect. *How to take a selfie infographic*. (2015). Retrieved from <http://www.frames-direct.com/landing/a/how-to-take-a-selfie.html>.

Frison, E., & Eggermont, S. (2016). Exploring the relationships between different types of Facebook use, perceived online social support, and adolescents' depressed mood. *Social*

Science Computer Review, 34(2), 153–171. Available from https://doi.org/10.1177/0894439314567449.

Frison, E., & Eggermont, S. (2017). Browsing, posting, and liking on Instagram: The reciprocal relationships between different types of Instagram use and adolescents' depressed mood. *Cyberpsychology, Behavior & Social Networking, 20*(10), 603–609. Available from https://doi.org/10.1089/cyber.2017.0156.

Gilbert, R., Murphy, N., & McNally, T. (2011). Addiction to the 3-dimesional internet: Estimated prevalence and relationship to real world addictions. *Addiction Research & Theory, 19*, 380–390. Available from https://doi.org/10.3109/16066359.2010.530714.

Griffiths, M. (2005). A "components" model of addiction within a biopsychosocial framework. *Journal of Substance Use, 10*, 191–197. Available from https://doi.org/10.1080/14659890500114359.

He, Q., Turel, O., & Bechara, A. (2017). Brain anatomy alterations associated with social networking site (SNS) addiction. *Scientific Reports, 7*, 1–8. (paper 45064).

Hong, F., Huang, D., Lin, H., & Chiu, S. (2014). Analysis of the psychological traits, Facebook usage, and Facebook addiction model of Taiwanese university students. *Telematics and Informatics, 31*, 597–606. Available from https://doi.org/10.1016/j.tele.2014.01.001.

Hormes, J. M., Kearns, B., & Alix Timko, C. (2014). Craving Facebook? Behavioral addiction to online social networking and its association with emotion regulation deficits. *Addiction, 109*, 2079–2088. Available from https://doi.org/10.1111/add.12713.

Horn, L. (2012). Study finds chemical reason behind Facebook 'addiction.' *PC Magazine, 1*, Retrieved from https://uk.pcmag.com/web-publishing/66544/study-finds-chemical-reason-behind-facebook-addiction.

Kaur, S., & Vig, D. (2016). Selfie and mental health issues: An overview. *Indian Journal of Health & Wellbeing, 7*(12), 1149–1152.

Kim, E., Lee, J. A., Sung, Y., & Choi, S. M. (2016). Predicting selfie-posting behavior on social networking sites: An extension of theory of planned behavior. *Computers in Human Behavior, 62*, 116–123.

Krasnova, H., Wenninger, H., Widjaja, T., & Buxmann, P. (2013). Envy on Facebook: A hidden threat to users' life satisfaction? In: *Paper presented at the 11th International Conference on Wirtschaftsinformatik.* Leipzig, Germany.

Kuss, D. J., Griffiths, M. D., Karila, L., & Billieux, J. (2014). Internet addiction: A systematic review of epidemiological research for the last decade. *Current Pharmaceutical Design, 20*, 4026–4052. Available from https://doi.org/10.2174/13816128113199990617.

Labrague, L. J. (2014). Facebook use and adolescents' emotional states of depression, anxiety, and stress. *Health Science Journal, 8*(1), 80–89.

Lenhart, A., Ling, R., Campbell, S., & Purcell, K. (2010). *Teens and mobile phones.* Washington, DC: Pew Internet & American Life Project.

Levenson, J., Shensa, A., Sidani, J. E., Colditz, J., & Primack, B. (2016). The association between social media use and sleep disturbance among young adults. *Preventive Medicine, 85*, 36–41.

Limayem, M., & Cheung, C. (2011). Predicting the continued use of Internet-based learning technologies: the role of habit. *Behaviour & Information Technology, 30*(1), 91–99. Available from https://doi.org/10.1080/0144929X.2010.490956.

Lin, L. Y., Sidani, J. E., Shensa, A., Radovic, A., Miller, E., Colditz, J. B., ... Primack, B. A. (2016). Association between social media use and depression among U.S. young adults. *Depression and Anxiety, 33*(4), 323–331. Available from https://doi.org/10.1002/da.22466.

Liu, T., & Potenza, M. (2007). Problematic Internet use: Clinical implications. *CNS Spectrums, 12*, 453–466. Available from https://doi.org/10.1017/S1092852900015339.

Longstreet, P., & Brooks, S. (2017). Life satisfaction: A key to managing internet & social media addiction. *Technology in Society*, *50*, 73–77. Available from https://doi.org/10.1016/j.techsoc.2017.05.003.

Lup, K., Trub, L., & Rosenthal, L. (2015). Instagram #instasad?: Exploring associations among Instagram use, depressive symptoms, negative social comparison, and strangers followed. *Cyberpsychology, Behavior, and Social Networking*, *18*, 247–252. Available from https://doi.org/10.1089/cyber.2014.0560.

Manago, A. M., Graham, M. B., Greenfield, P. M., & Salimkhan, G. (2008). Self-presentation and gender on MySpace. *Journal of Applied Developmental Psychology*, *29*(6), 446–458. Available from https://doi.org/10.1016/j.appdev.2008.07.001.

Mathers, C. D., & Loncar, D. (2006). Projections of global mortality and burden of disease from 2002 to 2030. *PLoS Medicine*, *3*(11), 2011–2030. Available from https://doi.org/10.1371/journal.pmed.0030442.

Mazer, J. P., & Ledbetter, A. M. (2012). Online communication attitudes as predictors of problematic internet usage and well-being outcomes. *Southern Communication Journal*, *77*, 403–419. Available from https://doi.org/10.1080/1041794X.2012.686558.

Medicinenet.com. (2014). Definition of serotonin. Retrieved from https://www.medicine-net.com/script/main/art.asp?articlekey = 5468.

Milani, L., Osualdella, D., & Di Blasio, P. (2009). Quality of interpersonal relationships and problematic Internet use in adolescence. *Cyberpsychology & Behavior*, *12*(6), 681–684. Available from https://doi.org/10.1089/cpb.2009.0071.

Moeller, S. (2010). *The world unplugged*. Retrieved from <http://theworldunplugged.word-press.com/addictions/>.

Moreno, M. A., Jelenchick, L. A., Koff, R., Eickhoff, J. C., Goniu, N., Davis, A., … Christakis, D. A. (2013). Associations between internet use and fitness among college students: An experience sampling approach. *Journal of Interaction Science*, *1*(4). Available from https://doi.org/10.1186/2194-0827-1-4.

Nabi, R. L., Prestin, A., & So, J. (2013). Facebook friends with (health) benefits? Exploring social network site use and perceptions of social support, stress, and well-being. *Cyberpsychology, Behavior, and Social Networking*, *10*, 721–727. Available from https://doi.org/10.1089/cyber.2012.0521.

Nolen-Hoeksema, S. (2000). The role of rumination in depressive disorders and mixed anxiety/depressive symptoms. *Journal of Abnormal Psychology*, *109*(3), 504–511.

Pal., S. (2015). *World mental health day-taking too many selfies is a mental disorder: Doctors*. Retrieved from <http://www.dnaindia.com>.

Pirkis, J. E., & Blood, W. (2010). *Suicide and the news and information media: A critical review*. Barton, ACT: Commonwealth of Australia.

Primack, B. A., Shensa, A., Escobar-Viera, C., Barrett, E. L., Sidani, J. E., Colditz, J. B., & James, E. (2017). Use of multiple social media platforms and symptoms of depression and anxiety: A nationally-representative study among U.S. young adults. *Computers in Human Behavior*, *69*, 1–9. Available from https://doi.org/10.1016/j.chb.2016.11.013.

Primack, B. A., Swanier, B., Georgiopoulos, A. M., Land, S. R., & Fine, M. J. (2009). Association between media use in adolescence and depression in young adulthood. *Archives of General Psychiatry*, *66*, 181. Available from https://doi.org/10.1001/archgenpsychiatry.2008.532.

Przybylski, A. K., Murayama, K., DeHaan, C. R., & Gladwell, V. (2013). Motivational, emotional, and behavioral correlates of fear of missing out. *Computers in Human Behavior*, *29*, 1841–1848. Available from https://doi.org/10.1016/j.chb.2013.02.014.

Qiu, L., Lu, J., Yang, S., Qu, W., & Zhu, T. (2015). What does your selfie say about you? *Computers in Human Behavior, 52*, 443–449.

Rosen, L.D., Cheever, N. A., & Carrier, L.M. (2012). *iDisorder: Understanding our obsession with technology and overcoming its hold on us.* New Your, NY: Palgrave Macmillan.

Savci, M., & Aysan, F. (2017). Technological addictions and social connectedness: Predictor effect of Internet addiction, social media addiction, digital game addiction and smartphone addiction on social connectedness. *Düşünen Adam: Journal of Psychiatry and Neurological Sciences, 30*(3), 202–216. Available from https://doi.org/10.5350/DAJPN2017300304.

Schaffer, H., Hall, M., & Bilt, J. V. (2000). Computer addiction: A critical consideration. *American Journal of Orthopsychiatry, 70*, 162–168. Available from https://doi.org/10.1037/h0087741.

Seabrook, E. M., Kern, M. L., & Rickard, N. S. (2016). Social networking sites, depression, and anxiety: A systematic review. *Journal of Medical Internet Research: Mental Health, 3*, e50. Available from https://doi.org/10.2196/mental.5842.

Shaw, A. M., Timpano, K. R., Tran, T. B., & Joormann, J. (2015). Correlates of Facebook usage patterns: The relationship between passive Facebook use, social anxiety symptoms, and brooding. *Computers in Human Behavior, 48*, 575–580.

Sheldon, P., & Bryant, K. (2016). Instagram: Motives for its use and relationship to narcissism and contextual age. *Computers in Human Behavior, 58*, 89–97. Available from https://doi.org/10.1016/j.chb.2015.12.059.

Sheldon, P., & Sykes, B. (2018). *Predictors of problematic social media use: Personality and lifeposition indicators.* Under review.

Shensa, A., Escobar-Viera, C. G., Sidani, J. E., Bowman, N. D., Marshal, M. P., & Primack, B. A. (2017). Problematic social media use and depressive symptoms among U.S. young adults: A nationally-representative study. *Social Science & Medicine, 182*, 150–157. Available from https://doi.org/10.1016/j.socscimed.2017.03.061.

Sidani, J. E., Shensa, A., Hoffman, B., Hanmer, J., & Primack, B. A. (2016). The association between social media use and eating concerns among US young adults. *Journal of the Academy of Nutrition & Dietetics, 116*(9), 1465–1472. Available from https://doi.org/10.1016/j.jand.2016.03.021.

Smahel, D., Wright, M. F., & Černíková, M. (2015). The impact of digital media on health: children's perspectives. *International Journal of Public Health, 60*, 131–137.

Sorokowski, P., Sorokowska, A., Oleszkiewicz, A., Frackowiak, T., Huk, A., & Pisanski, K. (2015). Selfie posting behaviors are associated with narcissism among men. *Personality and Individual Differences, 85*, 123–127.

Stefanone, M. A., Lackaff, D., & Rosen, D. (2011). Contingencies of self-worth and social-networking-site behavior. *Cyberpsychology, Behavior and Social Networking, 14*, 41–49. Available from https://doi.org/10.1089/cyber.2010.0049.

Stevens, S., Humphrey, K., Wheatley, T., & Galliher, R. V. (2011). Links among obsessive-compulsive personality characteristics and Facebook usage. *Psi Chi Journal of Undergraduate Research, 16*(3), 106–112.

Sung, Y., Lee, J. A., Kim, E., & Choi, S. M. (2016). Why we post selfies: Understanding motivations for posting pictures of oneself. *Personality and Individual Differences, 97*, 260–265.

Syed-Abdul, S., Fernandez-Luque, L., Jian, W., Li, Y., Crain, S., Hsu, M., ... Liou, D. (2013). Misleading health-related information promoted through video-based social media: Anorexia on YouTube. *Journal of Medical Internet Research, 15*(2), 137–149. Available from https://doi.org/10.2196/jmir.2237.

Tsitsika, A., Critselis, E., Louizou, A., Janikian, M., Freskou, A., Marangou, E., ... Kafetzis, D. (2011). Determinants of Internet addiction among adolescents: A case-control study. *The Scientific World Journal*, 11, 866–874.

Turel, O., & Serenko, A. (2012). The benefits and dangers of enjoyment with social networking websites. *European Journal of Information Systems*, 21(5), 512–528. Available from https://doi.org/10.1057/ejis.2012.1.

Twenge, J. M., Joiner, T. E., Rogers, M. L., & Martin, G. N. (2017). Increases in depressive symptoms, suicide-related outcomes, and suicide rates among U.S. adolescents after 2010 and links to increased new media screen time. *Clinical Psychological Science*, 6, 3–17. Available from https://doi.org/10.1177/2167702617723376.

Ueda, M., Mori, K., & Matsubayashi, T. (2014). The effects of media reports of suicides by well-known figures between 1989 and 2010 in Japan. *International Journal of Epidemiology*, 43(2), 623–629.

Ueda, M., Mori, K., Matsubayashi, T., & Sawada, Y. (2017). Tweeting celebrity suicides: Users' reaction to prominent suicide deaths on Twitter and subsequent increases in actual suicides. *Social Science & Medicine*, 189, 158–166. Available from https://doi.org/10.1016/j.socscimed.2017.06.032.

Valenzuela, S., Park, N., & Kee, K. F. (2009). Is there social capital in a social network site?: Facebook use and college students' life satisfaction, trust, and participation. *Journal of Computer-Mediated Communication*, 14(4), 875–901. Available from https://doi-org.elib.uah.edu/10.1111/j.1083-6101.2009.01474.x.

Vannucci, A., Flannery, K. M., & Ohannessian, C. M. (2017). Social media use and anxiety in emerging adults. *Journal of Affective Disorders*, 207, 163–166. Available from https://doi.org/10.1016/j.jad.2016.08.040.

van Rooij, A. J., Schoenmakers, T. M., van den Eijnden, R. M., Vermulst, A. A., & van de Mheen, D. (2012). Video game addiction test: Validity and psychometric characteristics. *Cyberpsychology, Behavior, and Social Networking*, 15(9), 507–511. Available from https://doi.org/10.1089/cyber.2012.0007.

Wang, J.-L., Jackson, L. A., Zhang, D.-J., & Su, Z.-Q. (2012). The relationships among Big Five personality factors, self-esteem, narcissism, and sensation-seeking to Chinese University students' uses of social networking sites (SNSs). *Computers in Human Behavior*, 28, 2313–2319.

Wang, P., Wang, X., Wu, Y., Xie, X., Wang, X., Zhao, F., ... Lei, L. (2018). Social networking sites addiction and adolescent depression: A moderated mediation model of rumination and self-esteem. *Personality and Individual Differences*, 127, 162–167. Available from https://doi.org/10.1016/j.paid.2018.02.008.

Watson, N. F., Badr, M. S., Belenky, G., Bliwise, D. L., Buxton, O. M., Buysse, D., ... Tasali, E. (2015). Recommended amount of sleep for a healthy adult: A joint consensus statement of the American Academy of Sleep Medicine and Sleep Research Society. *Journal of Clinical Sleep Medicine*, 11(8), 591–592.

Whipps, J., Byra, M., Gerow, K. G., & Guseman, E. H. (2018). Evaluation of nighttime media use and sleep patterns in first-semester college students. *American Journal of Health Behavior*, 42(3), 47–55. Available from https://doi.org/10.5993/AJHB.42.3.5.

Whiteford, H. A., Degenhardt, L., Rehm, J., Baxter, A. J., Ferrari, A. J., Erskine, H. E., ... Vos, T. (2013). Global burden of disease attributable to mental and substance use disorders: Findings from the Global Burden of Disease Study 2010. *The Lancet*, 382, 1575–1586. Available from https://doi.org/10.1016/S0140-6736(13)61611-6.

Wilkinson, P., Croudace, T., & Goodyer, I. M. (2013). Rumination, anxiety, depressive symptoms and subsequent depression in adolescents at risk for psychopathology: A longitudinal cohort study. *BMC Psychiatry*, 13(1), 60–78.

Wilson, K., Fornasier, S., & White, K. M. (2010). Psychological predictors of young adults' use of social networking sites. *Cyberpsychology, Behavior and Social Networking, 13,* 173—177. Available from https://doi.org/10.1089/cyber.2009.0094.

Woods, H. C., & Scott, H. (2016). #Sleepyteens: Social media use in adolescence is associated with poor sleep quality, anxiety, depression and low self-esteem. *Journal of Adolescence, 51,* 41—49. Available from https://doi.org/10.1016/j.adolescence.2016.05.008.

2

Narcissism as a Predictor of Self-Presentation

Ecclesiastes 2:11 "Then I considered all that my hands had done and the toil I had expended in doing it, and behold, all was vanity and a striving after wind, and there was nothing to be gained under the sun."

OUTLINE

The story of Narcissus derives from Greek mythology where Narcissus fell in love with his own image reflected in a pool of water. Some people believe narcissism is on the increase with the prevalence of technology and social media (Carpenter, 2012). Narcissism is the pursuit of gratification from vanity or egotistic admiration of one's own attributes. Since 1968, the American Psychiatric Association has listed narcissism in its Diagnostic and Statistical Manual of Disorders. Narcissism replaced the obsolete term of "megalomania." In this chapter, we will discuss generational differences in narcissism, intercultural distinctions, and types of narcissism including findings on platform usage involving Facebook, Instagram, and Twitter. We will conclude with a brief discussion on the Dark Triad of personality.

The study of narcissism began in the early twentieth century with the writings of Freud (1914), who examined personality and ego development. Narcissism has a diverse range of meanings, depending on whether it is used to describe a central concept of psychoanalytic theory, a mental illness, a social or cultural problem, or simply a personality trait (Campbell & Foster, 2007). Primary narcissism is the initial focus on the self with which all infants start and happens from around 6 months up to around 6 years. It is a defense mechanism that is used to protect the child from psychic damage during the formation of the individual self. Conversely, secondary narcissism is the more "normal" form, where older children and adults seek personal gratification over the achievement of social goals and conformance to social values. Common manifestations of this are bragging on social media. As Weiser (2015) articulates, social media is ideal for reinforcing narcissistic tendencies because it is a self-promotional platform, which allows exhibitionism and attention-seeking behaviors.

A degree of narcissism is common in many people. It becomes pathological when the narcissist lacks normal empathy and uses others ruthlessly to their own ends. As Honeycutt, Pence, and Gearhart (2013) note that with the exception of primary narcissism or healthy self-love, narcissism is often used to describe some kind of problem in a person or group's relationships with self and others. In everyday life, narcissism often means egoism, vanity, conceit, or simple selfishness. By definition, narcissism is an excessive love for one's self, feelings of superiority, and attention seeking (Vernon, Villani, Vickers, & Harris, 2008).

GENERATIONAL DIFFERENCES

Narcissism is considered a feature of contemporary culture and of recent generations (Twenge, 2007). Narcissism has increased over time (Grijalva et al., 2014; Twenge, Campbell, & Gentile, 2012) and popular media often credits this trend for the popularity of social media websites such as Facebook, Twitter, and Instagram. Some scholars report that approximately 70% of Millennials score higher on narcissism and lower on empathy than did the Gen X user of 30 years ago (Twenge & Foster, 2010).

Research by Roberts, Edmonds, and Grijalva (2010) shows that narcissism peaks during the years of young adulthood because self-centeredness appears to be a feature of that particular age period. Roberts and his associates concluded, after examining hundreds of studies over the past 30 years, that people in their 20s had the highest narcissistic scores. This is interesting to the extent that younger generations use social media more. Gen Z users (born between 2001 and 2017) have grown up with social media and 50% of these young users are on Instagram. Indeed, the first recognizable social media site was Six Degrees, which was created in 1997 and lasted until 2001 (Boyd & Ellison, 2007). About 70% of the Millennials (1981–2000) access Facebook, while 63% use YouTube. Gen X users (1965–80) have a strong social media presence. About 80% are on Facebook and Twitter, but only half have active accounts. As for the baby boomers (1946–64), Facebook is the most preferred social networking site (SNS). Of the 27 hours they spend online, 15.5% is spent on Facebook.

Other generational studies reveal that narcissism and Facebook use is correlated among Gen X users (Davenport, Bergman, Bergman, & Fearrington, 2014); especially the superiority (Panek, Nardis, & Konrath, 2013), vanity, exhibitionism, and exploitativeness (Leung, 2013) are the facets of narcissism. As noted, Millennials, or Generation Y, have lived an Internet-saturated existence for most of their lives (Tapscott, 1998; Twenge, 2007). In addition, some research indicates that Facebook is the preferred option for adults with narcissistic tendencies, while Twitter remains the platform of choice for younger narcissists (Weiser, 2015).

A metaanalysis of 80 studies examining the effect of self-esteem, narcissism, and loneliness on social media use reveals that across all generations social media use was higher among people low in self-esteem, high in narcissism, and high in loneliness (Liu & Baumeister, 2016). Interestingly, the links between narcissism and social media use were stronger in the Asian and collectivistic countries than in American and individualistic countries. McCain and Campbell (2016) review studies indicating how narcissism may be exhibited in a communal rather than agentic form in collectivistic countries (Gebauer, Sedikides, Verplanken, & Maio, 2012).

INTERCULTURAL DIFFERENCES IN NARCISSISM AND SOCIAL MEDIA USAGE

Social media usage differs between collectivistic and individualistic cultures. For example, Americans differ from Asian samples (e.g., Korean, Taiwanese, and Chinese) on the number of friends listed (Alhabash, Park, Kononova, Chiang, & Wise, 2012), topics discussed (Fong & Burton, 2008), and motivations reported (Kim, Sohn, & Choi, 2011) for using social media. Relatedly, Long and Zhang (2014) found independent self-construal (which is prevalent in individualistic cultures; Markus & Kitayama, 1991) to relate to differences between British (individualistic) and Japanese samples in motivations for social media use.

Cross-culturally, narcissism is correlated with Facebook usage. A study comparing Russian and German cultures reveal similar amounts of narcissism and self-presentation in both countries (Brailovskaiaa & Bierhoffb, 2016). However, German users posted more "Likes" and had more online-friends than Russian users, while Russians used more applications on Facebook than Germans. Hence, the positive association between narcissism, self-presentation, and social interaction on Facebook appear to be universal in Western and Eastern countries. Moreover, numerous studies reviewed by Honeycutt, Pence, and Gearhart (2014) indicate that the cross-cultural profile of a narcissist is the "lack perspective taking, indulge in fantasies, is disagreeable, neurotic, and open to new experiences, ruminates about conflict and does not compensate for the lack of conversational partners" (p. 344).

Some researchers have found that the use of first-person singular pronouns has increased in recent years (Twenge, Miller, & Campbell, 2014). These results reflect a cultural epidemic called "expressive individualism" that encourages persons to emphasize their own emotions and expressions instead of a general social structure. Social media could definitely be a contributing factor to the modern, self-absorbed culture.

In addition, research reveals that when Americans are compared to people from Pacific Rim cultures, such as Hong Kong, believe they are number one even though that is mathematically impossible (Singelis, Triandis, Bhawuk, & Gelfand, 1995). Vertical individualism is the cultural orientation where an autonomous self is valued but the individual self is perceived as different from and unequal to others. Superiority and competition are critical qualities of this orientation. The United States and France are examples of vertical individualism. According to Singelis, Triandis, and Bhawuk (1995), horizontal individualism is a cultural view in which an autonomous self is valued but the individual is more or less equal in status to others. Sweden and Australia are examples of horizontal collectivism. Horizontal collectivism is the cultural orientation in which the individual sees oneself as a member of an in-group whose members are similar to one another. However, the individual is dependent on others and equivalent to others. Equality is expected and practiced within this orientation. China is an example of horizontal collectivism. In the extreme, theoretical communism represents horizontal collectivism. Vertical collectivism is the cultural orientation in which a person views oneself as an important member of the in-group but the members are different from one another, in which some have more status than others. However, the self is interdependent, and inequality within the group is valued. In this orientation, serving and sacrifice are important. Japan, India, and rural traditional Greece are examples of vertical collectivism.

Cross-cultural research by McCann, Honeycutt, and Keaton (2010) reveals that Americans score higher on horizontal verticalism followed by the Japanese and Thai in descending order. Interestingly, there were no significant differences among the three groups on vertical individualism; where we might have expected the US students to score higher than the other groups. Some researchers claim that Americans flat out lie due to social desirability since it is vain to say that you feel you are more deserving of winning awards compared to peers (Triandis, Chen, & Chan, 1998). Finally, the Japanese scored higher on horizontal and vertical collectivism than the US and Thai students. Within each culture, the US students scored highest on horizontal individualism, then, in order, horizontal collectivism, vertical collectivism. Social media platforms reinforce these cultural differences.

TYPES OF NARCISSISM

Earlier, the differences between primary and secondary narcissisms were briefly noted. However, there are other types of narcissism which reflect different types of attraction. There are three types of attraction: task, social, and physical (Honeycutt & Sheldon, 2018). Respective examples are being attracted to someone who is competent at a skill or task (e.g., investment broker), being attracted to someone who is witty, funny, and conversationally involved, and being attracted to someone because of their looks. Cerebral narcissists derive their self-adoration from their intellectual abilities and achievements thus reflecting task absorption. Social narcissism is reflected by people who excessively think they are entertaining and good story-tellers. The pursuit of entertainment is associated with updating profile pictures containing a picture of one compared to something else as well as others liking the profile pictures (Wang, 2017). Twitter and Facebook offer an instantaneous platform to communicate their viewpoints. The fact that celebrities have so many "followers" reflects the vanity and shallowness of life in various cultures.

Somatic narcissists focus on the body, seeking beauty, physique and sexual conquests (physical obsession). Common examples are Hollywood celebrities endorsing products to enhance attraction as people age. There are cases of people who have undergone numerous plastic surgeries (e.g., over 50 surgeries and 100 cosmetic procedures and spending over $480,000) and who are so delusional that they want to look like Barbie and Ken dolls (Idov, 2017).

There are different traits associated with the Narcissistic Personality Inventory (NPI). For example, leadership ability is a positive trait while "grandiose exhibitionism" is bad and reflects being the center of attention, inappropriately disclosing, and saying shocking statements (Ackerman et al., 2011). Since these people cannot stand being ignored, their inclusion need is high in terms of interpersonal needs theory. Recall that the inclusion need is the need to be recognized and included in activities (Schutz, 1958). Social media allows lonely people to be included in a vast array of networks, activities, blogs, and forums. YouTube allows people to videotape themselves and advertise their interests to the cyber world.

A third type of narcissistic trait is the "entitlement/exploitativeness" dimension. Ackerman et al. (2011) argue this aspect includes "a sense of deserving respect and a willingness to manipulate and take advantage of others" (p. 6). People who are high in this trait show conceit and selfishness. More importantly, these people do not let the emotions and needs of others hinder their goals. Ackerman et al. (2011) found that participants with higher entitlement/exploitativeness scores were increasingly likely to have negative interactions reported by their roommate and their roommate was more likely to be dissatisfied with their relationship. In terms of exploitation, it has been found that narcissists respond more aggressively to derogatory comments made about them on Facebook's public walls (Carpenter, 2012).

Honeycutt et al. (2014) review the literature on the criticism of the Diagnostic and Statistical Manual of Mental Disorders (DSM) use of narcissism. For example, critics of the DSM criteria for narcissism say that it is too clinical and misses the more covert, hypersensitive, and vulnerable aspects of narcissistic disturbances (Wink, 1991). Part of this debate centers on the idea that people vary on a continuum from showing narcissistic tendencies to humility and selflessness. Research into characteristically narcissistic attribution styles has been over-reliant on the DSM-based measure of narcissism. However, Paulhus and Williams (2002) have refined items on the NPI to represent the nonclinical, everyday aspects of narcissism.

Covert narcissism is a distinct form of narcissism displayed by a person with a shy and introverted personality (Honeycutt et al., 2014; Paulhus & Williams, 2002). It is exemplified by grandiose fantasies and thoughts, a perception of entitlement, and a general sentiment of being better than others. Covert narcissism is expressed in a more passive and indirect manner than overt narcissism; it is conveyed with a condescending attitude, insincerity, passive aggressiveness, defensiveness, and hostility. People have these traits in varying degrees indicating its normalcy.

Hendin and Cheek (1997) found that a person can be vulnerable and self-absorbed simultaneously. For example, they found that covert narcissism has a strong negative association with agreeableness ($r = -0.44$) and is positively correlated with neuroticism ($r = 0.55$). The magnitude of these correlations is high and informative because neuroticsm may be related to increased social media usage. Some research reveals that neuroticism is associated with the use of Facebook followed by the use of Google +, Twitter, MySpace, and Skype in descending order (Lahari, 2014). Yet, other research has revealed that only extraversion and openness were associated with social media usage (Alan & Kabaday, 2016). The contradictory results can be explained in terms of methodology, including how the personality traits were measured, and large differences in sample sizes (Range 100–500).

Honeycutt et al. (2013) found relationships between antisocial traits in the form of neuroticism, lack of conscientiousness, and imagined interactions. Imagined interactions are a type of social cognition and daydreaming in which people use visual and verbal imagery with significant others including Facebook friends that serve a variety of functions including catharsis (Honeycutt, 2003, 2015). Antisocial traits have been referred to as the dark triad. The dark triad consists of Machiavellianism, narcissism, and psychopathy. Machiavellians, narcissists, and psychopaths have a tendency to manipulate and exploit others to get what they desire (Lee, Ashton, & Shin, 2005). Machiavellians are characterized by manipulation and exploitation of others with a mocking disregard for morality and a focus on self-interest and deception (Jakobwitz & Egan, 2006). Machiavellianism reflects a tendency to deceive and manipulate other people for gain (Anglo, 2005). The narcissistic personality is characterized by a pretentious self-concept, a sense of entitlement, lack of empathy, and consideration. The psychopath, or antisocial personality, is characterized by impulsive thrill-seeking and selfishness, insensitivity, lack of emotion, superficial charm, and remorselessness (Paulhus & Williams, 2002).

Despite the similarities between these three personalities, research has revealed that they are distinct personalities (Paulhus & Williams, 2002). For example, Machiavellian's are different from narcissists in that they do not make exaggerated claims about their importance and do not strive to impress others. A second example is that Machiavellian's and narcissists differ from psychopaths in that these individuals can understand the emotions of others and can express empathy for their victims (Christie & Geis, 1970).

Sanecka (2017) found that all three Dark Triad components are positively associated with posting and editing selfies on SNSs. However, regression analysis demonstrated that only narcissism predicted selfie-related behaviors. Narcissism and Machiavellianism are positively related to the amount of personal information disclosed online and the tendency to self-disclose intentionally in computer-mediated communication.

FACEBOOK USE AND NARCISSISM

Numerous studies reveal the association between narcissism and frequency of using Facebook (e.g., Buffardi & Campbell, 2008; Mehdizadeh, 2010; Ong et al., 2011). In addition the more friends that a user has in his/her network, the higher their scores on measures of narcissism (Bergman, Fearrington, Davenport, & Bergman, 2011). Hall (2017) discusses how narcissists use social media to project perfectionism. She writes the following:

> Users of social media, by and large, want to show a good face, but the narcissist seeks to project perfection and can't resist the compulsion to outshine her peers. To appear popular, she may attempt to collect large numbers of "friends" and "followers" even if the vast majorities are surface acquaintances or strangers. She tends to post often and show idealized images of herself and her life. She may regularly feature flattering close-ups of her face or images that highlight her best physical qualities. She will often post images of herself on vacation, traveling, socializing, or attending important events to cultivate the perception that she is living "the high life." Table 2.1 presents various characteristics of narcissistic use of social media that are summarized across various studies (e.g., McCain & Campbell, 2016).

> A smartphone data-tracking study analyzed how much time people spent on mobile every day and found that participants with higher smartphone usage typically have lower scores on the NPI. According to the authors, this can be explained by the fact that people mostly use their smartphones for social interaction, which is exactly what narcissists avoid (Reid & Thomas, 2017). Interestingly, people who score high on the NPI report more friends

TABLE 2.1 Characteristics of Narcissists Using Social Media

Characteristic

1. Pretending perfection—Attempt to have large number of friends & followers even if they are superficial strangers
2. Visual socialization—Posting many images of oneself socializing with others
3. Self-centeredness—Desires others to like his/her posts, but is less inclined to like other's post
4. Vanity—Show more attractive photos with flattering facial close-ups to show the best physical qualities
5. Family members are pictured as minor actors in which the self is the lead
6. May prefer Twitter due to the instantaneous and dissemination of news and accumulating followers without following others
7. Online trolling—Need to be dominant; can be shown attacking others with whom they disagree with
8. Higher frequency of status updates
9. Write more autobiographical information about themselves in the "About" section
10. Use more profane and antisocial words in posts

Note: Summarized from Hall (2017) and McCain and Campbell (2016), also see Sanecka (2017).

on Facebook, tagged themselves more often, changed their photos frequently, were self-promoting, and updated their newsfeeds more regularly (Carpenter, 2012). As noted throughout this chapter, this is a recurring finding.

Research reveals that narcissists use more profane and antisocial terms. For example, a linguistic analysis of 1000 Twitter accounts revealed that people with higher levels of narcissism were found to use more words about anger and negative emotions and fewer words about social interaction (Golbeck, 2016). Indeed, Marshall, Lefringhausen, and Ferenczi (2015) in a study of over 550 Facebook users report that narcissists' used Facebook for attention-seeking and validation of their views. Hence, they often updated their accomplishments including diet and exercise. The tendency to update their trivial accomplishments explained the greater number of likes and comments that they reported receiving to their updates. They also found that Extraverts more frequently updated about their social activities and openness was correlated with updating about intellectual topics, while self-esteem was negatively associated with updating about romantic partners.

Research on self-esteem and social comparison theory is interesting. Social comparison theory explains how people compare themselves to other people in order to develop their self-concept. For example, I will feel better about myself if I compare myself to someone whom I perceive as inferior. This reflects a downward comparison. Conversely, if I compare myself to someone who is superior such as a mentor, this is an upward comparison. Self-comparisons affect the way we deal with our emotions, decision-making decisions, and receive feedback from others (Vogel, Rose, Roberts, & Eckles, 2014). Social media offers a vast array of social comparison since you can compare yourself cross culturally. While people who used Facebook often had lower self-esteem; this finding was even lower for social media users who were exposed to profiles designed to facilitate upward social comparisons (Vogel et al., 2014). Indeed, social media platforms function nicely with social comparison theory because it is so much easier comparing yourself to the "ideal."

NARCISSISM AND INSTAGRAM

Research on the dark side of social media in terms of Instagram among college students reveals a positive association between narcissism and the use of Instagram for surveillance and popularity purposes (Honeycutt & Sheldon, 2018; Sheldon & Bryant, 2016). Narcissism is positively associated with the amount of time that participants spend editing photos before posting them on Instagram. A study of middle and high school students ranging in age from 12 to 17 revealed that narcissism was the most important predictor of Instagram use compared to other personality variables (Honeycutt & Sheldon, 2018). Among teens, "selfies," or photographs that users take of themselves with a smartphone, are very popular on Instagram. Selfies have been described as a symptom of social media–driven narcissism (Weiser, 2015). Research reveals that narcissism scores are significantly higher among young adults in the 2000s than they were in the 1980s and 1990s (Twenge, Konrath, Foster, Campbell, & Bushman, 2008).

Narcissists "like" fellow narcissists on Instagram as revealed in a study of 276 Instagram users (Paramboukis, Skues, & Wise, 2016). They examined grandiose narcissism and vulnerable narcissism. Grandiose narcissism is characterized by exhibitionism, callousness, extraversion, manipulativeness, superiority, aggression, indifference, and seeking of acclaim (Ackerman et al., 2011). Conversely, vulnerable narcissism reflects inadequacy, emptiness, shame, reactive anger, helplessness, hypervigilance to insult, excessive shyness, and interpersonal avoidance (Miller & Campbell, 2008).

Paramboukis et al. (2016) discovered that both types of narcissists were more likely to engage in attention-seeking behavior on Instagram such as hash tagging expensive products, posting photos of things you desire but do not have, and posting photos of celebrities that you admire. Neither group was likely to engage in empathetic behavior like shout outs. However, vulnerable narcissists were more likely to post pictures of themselves at impressive events as well as posting request for followers. Vulnerable narcissists using Instagram as a platform to seek out positive reinforcement aligns with the notion that people seek validation from others in order to boost self-esteem Indeed, another study found that pictures with human faces are 38% more likely to be liked and 32% more likely to be commented on (Bakhshi, Shamma, & Gilbert, 2014).

Paramboukis et al. (2016) found that Narcissists who post selfies to Instagram are more likely to follow "arrogant" and "attention-seeking" users reflecting reciprocity. This study also found that 64% of Millennials believe Instagram is the most narcissistic social media platform. This was followed by Snapchat (15%), Twitter (11%), and Facebook (10%). Notice, how the other platforms when combined (36%) dwindle in comparison to Instagram narcissism. They concluded that Instagram is a medium for expressing existing narcissistic tendencies rather than a platform that encourages or causes extremes of narcissistic behavior. Two-thirds of Millennials admitted to liking photos and videos from people who had previously liked their own posts.

NARCISSISM AND TWITTER

While narcissism is associated with social media usage in various genres as noted above, it is especially associated with Twitter usage. This section will review various findings. It is too bad that we cannot tweet these results as we are writing this for more narcissistic coverage. McKinney, Kelley, and Duran (2012) argue that Twitter is a good venue for narcissists because it allows them to answer the question, "What are you doing?" in terms of 140 characters or less. Followers are supposedly interested in one's moment-to-moment postings, which suggests egocentrism, self-aggrandizement, and self-importance—the very characteristics of narcissistic individuals. Their study revealed that being open about sharing information about oneself was significantly related to the frequency of using Facebook and Twitter to provide self-focused updates, while high scores on narcissism were associated with a larger number of Facebook friends and with the number of self-focused "tweets" that people send. In addition, posting selfies on social media is another reflection of narcissism (Murray, 2015).

The Big Five personality traits are stable, primordial personality traits that consist of neuroticism, openness, conscientiousness, extraversion, and agreeableness (Cobb-Clark & Schurer, 2012; Honeycutt et al., 2013; McCrae & Terracciano, 2005). Openness reflects the degree of intellectual curiosity, creativity, and preference for novelty and variety. Conscientiousness is the predisposition to show self-discipline and refers to planning, organization, and dependability. Extraversion reflects the need to seek stimulation in the company of others, sociability, and talkativeness. Agreeableness is the tendency to be compassionate and cooperative towards others. Finally, neuroticism reveals the tendency to experience negative emotions such as anger, anxiety, depression, or vulnerability. Neuroticism reflects emotional stability and control of impulses.

McCain and Campbell (2016) summarize a few findings on the Big Five traits and social media usage. They indicate how the traits associated with narcissism reflect a trait model of narcissism as opposed to a state or situational model in which people are narcissistic in some platforms and less narcissistic in others. In Big Five terms, grandiose narcissism is associated with high levels of extraversion and openness and low levels of agreeableness (Miller et al., 2011). Extraverts have larger social networks in general (Pollet, Roberts, & Dunbar, 2011; Roberts, Wilson, Fedurek, & Dunbar, 2008) and spend more time and generate more content on social media sites (Gosling, Augustine, Vazire, Holtzman, & Gaddis, 2011). Thus narcissists' tendency to have more friends and generate more content on social media may be associated with their extraversion. Conversely, vulnerable narcissism is associated with low agreeableness and neuroticism. These findings suggest that anxiety is associated with increased social media usage.

Qiu, Lin, Ramsay, and Yang (2012) measured the "Big Five" personality traits of openness, conscientiousness, extraversion, agreeableness, and neuroticism among 142 Twitter users. They analyzed their participants' tweets over a month-long period and used a software program called Linguistic Inquiry and Word Count to look for patterns in the language they used. They found that extraverts used more assent words, fewer functional words, and fewer impersonal pronouns. Openness was negatively related to the use of adverbs, swear words, affect words, and nonfluent words, but positively related to prepositions. When Qiu and his colleagues asked those who had never met the Twitter users to judge their personalities based only on their Twitter feeds, they found that people could accurately judge two of the Big Five dimensions—neuroticism and agreeableness.

THE DARK TRIAD OF PERSONALITY

Narcissism is one of the three traits that make up the "dark triad of personality." The dark triad consists of Machiavellianism, narcissism, and psychopathy. Machiavellians, narcissists, and psychopaths have a tendency to manipulate and exploit others to get what they desire (Lee, & Ashton, & Shin, 2005). Machiavellians are characterized by manipulation and exploitation of others, with a mocking disregard for morality and a focus on self-interest and deception (Jakobwitz & Egan, 2006). Machiavellianism reflects a tendency to deceive and manipulate other people for gain (Anglo, 2005). The narcissistic personality is characterized by a pretentious self-concept, a sense of entitlement, lack of empathy, and consideration while the psychopath, or antisocial personality, is characterized by impulsive thrill-seeking and selfishness, insensitivity, lack of emotion, superficial charm, and remorselessness (Paulhus & Williams, 2002).

Users high in narcissism have Twitter profile images that are less likely to be grayscale and more likely to feature a single, smiling face (Preotiuc-Pietro, Carpenter, Giorgi, & Ungar, 2016). These profiles reflect a desire to present oneself positively and be the center of attention. Furthermore, in terms of profile features, narcissism was positively associated with geo-enabled tweets—suggesting Twitter use from mobile—and it was negatively associated with duplicate posts. Their data revealed that psychopathy was associated with the use of angry and violent ("killed," "injuries," and "furious") posts. They concluded that Narcissists tweet about prosaic events with the appearance of positivity, while psychopaths tweet about violence and death with angry emotion. In terms of Machiavellianism, their results reveal Twitter users who are high in the trait post fewer URLs and fewer retweets.

Honeycutt and Sheldon (2018) review numerous studies indicating that narcissists prefer cyber communities consisting of superficial relationships because they have control over their self-presentation. Narcissists believe that they are better than others, unique, and special (Leung, 2013).

The most important indicators of narcissism on Facebook are the main profile photo and the number of social contacts (Buffardi & Campbell, 2008). Narcissists are highly motivated to choose profile photos that emphasize their attractiveness (Kapidzic, 2013). Those who score higher on narcissism update their Facebook statuses more often and also self-disclose more (Winter et al., 2014). Self-disclosure is their strategy to increase attention to themselves.

Sheldon (2016) found that college students who score higher on narcissism are liking, commenting, and uploading their own photos on Facebook more often than those who score lower on narcissism. For narcissists these activities might be a way of self-presentation. When a person "likes" or responds on somebody else's photos, the friends of the person who liked them will get the newsfeed notification of the activity. As Greenwood, Stefancic, and Tsemberis (2013) argued, one of the psychological needs individuals have includes the need to be "seen."

SUMMARY AND CONCLUSION

Different types of narcissism are paramount in contemporary society. The current generation has more narcissistic tendencies than earlier generations. Indeed, the link between narcissism and social media behavior reflects a pattern of a self-reinforcing spiral (Gnambs & Appel, 2017). Hence, various types of narcissistic tendencies affect the use of social media activities which reinforce the disposition. Essentially, narcissistic tendencies and social media platform behaviors feed off each other. Hence, due to social media access, there are abundant examples everyday of self-indulgence. Before this access existed, people had limited information sources. Even popular entertainment, like reality shows, is visual examples of grandiose narcissism. Who is following whom? Grandiose narcissists are encountered more frequently in social networks than vulnerable narcissists. Moreover, an association has been found between the number of friends a person has and how many photos they upload and the prevalence of traits associated with narcissism. Indeed, social media feeds some aspects of the Dark Triad of personality including neuroticism. Additional research needs to explore what the narcissists do and how they cope when the "plug is pulled" due to power and electrical grid outages. Relatedly, the next chapter explores the dark side of cyberstalking. It is possible that some narcissists may cyberstalk since rejection reflects a type of criticism.

References

Ackerman, R. A., Witt, E. A., Donnellan, M. B., Trzesniewski, K. H., Robins, R. W., & Kashy, D. A. (2011). What does the narcissistic personality inventory really measure? *Assessment, 18*, 67–87. Available from https://doi.org/10.1177/1073191110382845.

Alan, A. K., & Kabaday, E. T. (2016). The effect of personal factors on social media usage of young consumers. *Procedia—Social and Behavioral Sciences, 235*, 595–602. Available from https://doi.org/10.1016/j.sbspro.2016.11.086.

Alhabash, S., Park, H., Kononova, A., Chiang, Y.-h, & Wise, K. (2012). Exploring the motivations of Facebook use in Taiwan. *Cyberpsychology, Behavior, and Social Networking, 15* (6), 304–311. Available from https://doi.org/10.1089/cyber.2011.0611.

Anglo, S. (2005). *Machiavelli: The First Century*. Oxford, England: Oxford University Press, 2005.

Bakhshi, S., Shamma, D. A., & Gilbert, E. (2014). Faces engage us: Photos with faces attract more likes and comments on Instagram. In *Proceedings of the SIGCHI conference on human factors in computing systems*. <https://doi.org/10.1145/2556288.2557403>.

Bergman, S. M., Fearrington, M. E., Davenport, S. W., & Bergman, J. Z. (2011). Millennials, narcissism, and social networking: What narcissists do on social networking sites and why. *Personality and Individual Differences, 50*(5), 706–711. Available from https://doi.org/10.1016/j.paid.2010.12.022.

Boyd, D. M., & Ellison, N. B. (2007). Social network sites: Definition, history, and scholarship. *Journal of Computer-Mediated Communication, 13*(1), 210−230. Available from https://doi.org/10.1111/j.1083-6101.2007.00393.x.

Brailovskaiaa, J., & Bierhoffb, H. W. (2016). Cross-cultural narcissism on Facebook: Relationship between self-presentation, social interaction and the open and covert narcissism on a social networking site in Germany and Russia. *Computers in Human Behavior, 55*, 251−257. Available from https://doi.org/10.1016/j.chb.2015.09.018.

Buffardi, L. E., & Campbell, W. K. (2008). Narcissism and social networking websites. *Personality and Social Psychology Bulleting, 34*, 1303−1314.

Campbell, W. K., & Foster, J. D. (2007). The narcissistic self: Background, an extended agency model, and ongoing controversies. In C. Sedikides, & S. Spencer (Eds.), *Frontiers in social psychology: The self* (pp. 115−162). Philadelpha, PA: Psychology Press.

Carpenter, C. J. (2012). Narcissism on Facebook: Self-promotional and anti-social behavior. *Personality and Individual Differences, 52*, 482−486. Available from https://doi.org/10.1016/j.paid.2011.11.011.

Christie, R., & Geis, F. (1970). *Studies in Machiavellianism*. NY, NY: Academic Press.

Cobb-Clark, D. A., & Schurer, S. (2012). The stability of big-five personality traits. *Economics Letters, 115*(2), 11−15.

Davenport, S. W., Bergman, S. M., Bergman, J. Z., & Fearrington, M. E. (2014). Twitter versus Facebook: Exploring the role of narcissism in the motives and usage of different social media platforms. *Computers in Human Behavior, 32*, 212−220. https://doi.org/10.1016/j.chb.2013.12.011. Version of record available from: www.elsevier.com.

Freud, S. (1914). On Narcissism. In *The standard edition of the complete psychological works of Sigmund Freud, Volume XIV (1914−1916): On the History of the Psycho-Analytic Movement, papers on metapsychology and other works* (pp. 67−102).

Fong, J., & Burton, S. (2008). A cross-cultural comparison of electronic word-of-mouth and country-of-origin effects. *Journal of Business Research, 61*, 233−242. Available from https://doi.org/10.1016/j.jbusres.2007.06.015.

Gebauer, J. E., Sedikides, C., Verplanken, B., & Maio, G. R. (2012). Communal narcissism. *Journal of Personality and Social Psychology, 103*(5), 854−878. Available from https://doi.org/10.1037/a0029629.

Gnambs, T., & Appel, M. (2017). Narcissism and social networking behavior: A meta-analysis. *Journal of Personality*. Available from https://doi.org/10.1111/jopy.12305, online.

Greenwood, R. M., Stefancic, A., & Tsemberis, S. (2013). Pathways housing first for homeless persons with psychiatric disabilities: Program innovation, research, and advocacy. *Journal of Social Issues, 69*(4), 645−663. Available from https://bobcat.militaryfamilies.psu.edu/sites/default/files/placed-programs/Greenwood%20&%20Tsemberis,%202013_program%20information.pdf.

Golbeck, J. (2016). Negativity and anti-social attention seeking among narcissists on Twitter: A linguistic analysis. *First Monday, 21*(3). Available from https://doi.org/10.5210/fm.v0i0.6017.

Gosling, S. D., Augustine, A. A., Vazire, S., Holtzman, N., & Gaddis, S. (2011). Manifestations of personality in Online Social Networks: self-reported Facebook-related behaviors and observable profile information. *Cyberpsychology, behavior and social networking, 14*(9), 483−488. https://doi.org/10.1089/cyber.2010.0087.

Grijalva, E., Newman, D., Tay, L., Donnellan, M. B., Harms, P. D., Robins, R. W., & Yan, T. (2014). Gender differences in narcissism: A meta-analytic review. *Psychological Bulletin, 141*, 261−310.

Hall, J. L. (2017). The narcissist on social media: The exhibitionist and troll. *The Narcissist Family Files*. Retrieved on March 23, 2018 from http://narcissistfamilyfiles.com/2017/05/01/the-narcissist-on-social-media-the-exhibitionist-and-troll/.

Hendin, H. M., & Cheek, J. M. (1997). Assessing hypersensitive narcissism: A re-examination of Murray's narcissism scale. *Journal of Research in Personality, 31,* 588–599. Available from https://doi.org/10.1006/jrpe.1997.2204.

Honeycutt, J. M., Pence, M. E., & Gearhart, C. (2014). Associations between narcissism, empathy, personality, and imagined interactions. In A. Besser (Ed.), *Handbook of the psychology of narcissism: Diverse perspectives* (pp. 333–346). Nork: Nova Science.

Honeycutt, J. M. (2003). *Imagined interactions: Daydreaming about communication.* Hampton, Brunswick, NJ.

Honeycutt, J. M. (2015). Imagined interaction theory: Mental representations of interpersonal communication. In D. O. Braithwaite, & P. Schrodt (Eds.), *Engaging Theories in Interpersonal* Communication (2nd ed, pp. 75–87). Thousand Oaks, CA: Sage.

Honeycutt, J. M., Pence, M. E., & Gearhart, C. C. (2013). Using imagined interactions to predict covert narcissism. *Communication Reports, 26,* 26–38. Available from https://doi.org/10.1080/08934215.2013.773051.

Honeycutt, J. M., & Sheldon, P. (2018). *Scripts and communication for relationships* (2nd ed.). NY: Peter Lang.

Idov, M. (2017). *This is not a Barbie Doll. This is an actual human being.* Retrieved from: <https://www.gq.com/story/valeria-lukyanova-human-barbie-doll>.

Jakobwitz, S., & Egan, V. (2006). The dark triad and normal personality traits. *Personality and Individual Differences, 40*(2), 331–339. Available from https://doi.org/10.1016/j.paid.2005.07.006.

Kapidzic, S. (2013). Narcissism as a predictor of motivations behind facebook profile picture selection. *Cyberpsychology, Behavior, and Social Networking, 22,* 14–19. Available from https://doi.org/10.1089/cyber.2012.0143.

Kim, Y., Sohn, D., & Choi, S. M. (2011). Cultural difference in motivations for using social network sites: A comparative study of American and Korean college students. *Computers in Human Behavior, 27*(1), 365–372. Available from https://doi.org/10.1016/j.chb.2010.08.015.

Lahari, D. H. (2014). Study of neuroticism on usage and preference of social networking sites as a function of educational background and gender. *International Journal of Research in Humanities, Arts and Literature, 2,* 91–96. Retrieved from: http://www.impactjournals.us/download.php?fname=2-11-1405758923-12.%20Humanities-Study%20of%20Newroticism%20on%20usage%20and%20preference%20of%20social-Dinesh%20Kumar%20Lahari.pdf.

Lee, K., Ashton, M. C., & Shin, K.-H. (2005). Personality Correlates of Workplace Anti-Social Behavior. *Applied Psychology: An International Review, 54*(1), 81–98. Available from https://doi.org/10.1111/j.1464-0597.2005.00197.x.

Leung, L. (2013). Generational differences in content generation in social media: The roles of the gratifications sought and of narcissism. *Computers in Human Behavior, 29,* 997–1006. Available from https://www.dhi.ac.uk/san/waysofbeing/data/economy-crone-leung-2013.pdf.

Liu, D., & Baumeister, R. F. (2016). Social networking online and personality of self-worth: A meta-analysis. *Journal of Research in Personality, 64,* 79–89. Available from https://doi.org/10.1016/j.jrp.2016.06.024.

Long, K., & Zhang, X. (2014). *Cyberpsychology, Behavior, and Social Networking, 17,* 454–459. Available from https://doi.org/10.1089/cyber.2013.0506.

Marshall, T. C., Lefringhausen, K., & Ferenczi, N. (2015). The big five, self-esteem, and narcissism as predictors of the topics people write about in Facebook status updates. *Personality and Individual Differences, 85,* 35–40. Available from https://doi.org/10.1016/j.paid.2015.04.039.

Markus, H. R., & Kitayama, S. (1991). Culture and the self: Implications for cognition, emotion, and motivation. *Psychological Review, 98*(2), 224–253. Available from https://doi.org/10.1037/0033-295X.98.2.224.

McCain, J., & Campbell, W. K. (2016). Narcissism and social media use: A meta-analytic review. *Psychology of Popular Media Culture*. Available from https://doi.org/10.1037/ppm0000137.

McCann, R. M., Honeycutt, J. M., & Keaton, S. A. (2010). Toward greater specificity in cultural value analyses: The interplay of intrapersonal communication affect and cultural values in Japan, Thailand, and the United States. *Journal of Intercultural Communication Research, 39*(3), 157–172. Available from https://doi.org/10.1080/17475759.2010.534862.

McCrae, R. R., & Terracciano, A. (2005). Personality profiles of cultures: Aggregate personality traits. *Journal of Personality and Social Psychology, 89*(3), 407–425. Available from https://doi.org/10.1037/0022-3514.89.3.407.

McKinney, B. C., Kelley, L., & Duran, R. L. (2012). Narcissism or openness? College students' use of Facebook and Twitter. *Communication Research Reports, 29,* 108–118. Available from https://doi.org/10.1080/08824096.2012.666919.

Mehdizadeh, S. (2010). Self-presentation 2.0: Narcissism and self-esteem on Facebook. *Cyberpsychology, Behavior, and Social Networking, 13,* 357–364.

Miller, J. D., & Campbell, K. (2008). Comparing clinical and social personality conceptualizations of narcissism. *Journal of Personality, 76,* 449–476. Available from https://doi.org/10.1111/j.1467-6494.2008.00492.x, 3514.89.3.407.

Miller, J. D., Hoffman, B. J., Gaughan, E. T., Gentile, B., Maples, J., & Campbell, K. (2011). Grandiose and vulnerable narcissism: a nomological network analysis. *Journal of Personality, 79*(5), 1013–1042. Available from https://www.doi.org/10.1111/j.1467-6494.2010.00711.x.

Murray, D. C. (2015). Notes to self: The visual culture of selfies in the age of social media. *Consumption Markets, & Culture, 18,* 490–516. Available from https://doi.org/10.1080/10253866.2015.1052967.

Ong, E. Y. L., Ang, R. P., Ho, J. C. M., Lim, J. C. Y., Goh, D. H., Lee, C. S., et al. (2011). Narcissism, Extraversion, and adolescents' self-presentation on Facebook. *Personality and Individual Differences* (50, pp. 180–185).

Panek, E. T., Nardis, Y., & Konrath, S. (2013). Mirror or Megaphone?: How relationships between narcissism and social networking site use differ on Facebook and Twitter. *Computers in Human Behavior, 29,* 2004–2012. Available from https://doi.org/10.1016/j.chb.2013.04.012.

Paramboukis, O., Skues, J., & Wise, L. (2016). An exploratory study of the relationships between narcissism, self-esteem and Instagram use. *Social Networking, 5,* 82–92. Available from https://doi.org/10.4236/sn.2016.52009.

Paulhus, D. L., & Williams, K. M. (2002). The dark triad of personality: Narcissism, Machiavellianism, and psychopathy. *Journal of Research in Personality, 36,* 556–563. Available from https://doi.org/10.1016/S0092-6566(02)00505.

Preotiuc-Pietro, D., Carpenter, J., Giorgi, S., & Ungar, L. (2016). Studying the Dark triad of personality through twitter behavior. In *CIKM '16 Proceedings of the 25th ACM international on conference on information and knowledge management* (pp. 761–770). <https://doi.org/10.1145/2983323.2983822>.

Pollet, T. V., Roberts, S. G. B., & Dunbar, R. I. M. (2011). Use of Social Network Sites and Instant Messaging Does Not Lead to Increased Offline Social Network Size, or to Emotionally Closer Relationships with Offline Network Members. *Cyberpsychology, Behavior, and Social Networking, 14,* 253–258. Available from https://doi.org/10.1089/cyber.2010.0161p.

Qiu, L., Lin, H., Ramsay, J. E., & Yang, G. (2012). You are what you tweet: Personality expression and perception on Twitter. *Journal of Research in Personality, 46*, 710–718. Available from https://doi.org/10.1016/j.jrp.2012.08.008.

Reid, A. J., & Thomas, C. N. (2017). A case study in smartphone usage and gratification in the age of narcissism. *International Journal of Technology and Human Interaction, 13*(2), 40–56. Available from https://doi.org/10.4018/IJTHI.2017040103.

Roberts, B. W., Edmonds, G., & Grijalva, E. (2010). It is developmental me, not generation me: developmental changes are more important than generational changes in narcissism-commentary on Trzesniewski & Donnellan (2010). *Perspectives on Psychological Science, 5* (1), 97–102. Available from https://doi.org/10.1177/1745691609357019.

Roberts, S. G. B., Wilson, R., Fedurek, P., & Dunbar, R. I. M. (2008). Individual differences and personal social network size and structure. *Personality and Individual Differences, 44* (4), 954–964. Available from https://doi.org/10.1016/j.paid.2007.10.033.

Sanecka, E. (2017). The dark side of social media: Associations between the dark triad of personality, self-disclosure online and selfie-related behaviors. *Journal of Education Culture and Society, 7*(2), 71–88. Available from https://jecs.pl/index.php/jecs/article/view/10.15503.jecs20172.71.88.

Schutz, W. C. (1958). *FIRO:* A three-dimensional theory of interpersonal behavior. Oxford, England: Rinehart.

Sheldon, P. (2016). Self-monitoring, covert narcissism, and sex as predictors of self-presentational activities on Facebook. *The Journal of Social Media in Society* (5, pp. 70–91).

Sheldon, P., & Bryant, K. (2016). Instagram: Motives for its use and relationship to narcissism and contextual age. *Computers in Human Behavior, 58*, 89–97. Available from https://doi.org/10.1016/j.chb.2015.12.059.

Singelis, T., Triandis, H., Bhawuk, D., & Gelfand, M. (1995). Horizontal and vertical individualism and collectivism: a theoretical and measurement refinement. *Cross-cultural Research, 29*, 240–275. Available from https://doi.org/10.1177/106939719502900302.10.1177/106939719502900302.

Triandis, H. C., Chen, X. P., & Chan, D. K. S. (1998). Scenarios for the measurement of collectivism and individualism. *Journal of Cross-Cultural Psychology, 29*, 275–289. Available from https://doi.org/10.1177/0022022198292001.

Tapscott, D. (1998). *Growing Up Digital. The Rise of the Net Generation.* NY, NY: McGraw Hill, 2008.

Twenge, J. M. (2007). *Generation me.* New York: Atria Books.

Twenge, J. M., Campbell, W. K., & Gentile, B. (2012). Generational increases in agentic self-evaluations among American college students, 1966–2009. *Self and Identity, 11*, 409–427.

Twenge, J. M., & Foster, J. D. (2010). Birth cohort increases in narcissistic personality traits among American college students, 1982–2009. *Social Psychological and Personality Science, 5*, 227–229.

Twenge, J. M., Konrath, S., Foster, J., Campbell, W., & Bushman, B. (2008). Egos inflating over time: A cross-temporal meta-analysis of the narcissistic personality inventory. *Journal of Personality, 76*(4), 875–928. Available from https://doi.org/10.1111/j.1467-6494.2008.00507.x.

Twenge, J. M., Miller, J. D., & Campbell, W. K. (2014). The narcissism epidemic: Commentary on modernity and narcissistic personality disorder. *Personality Disorders, 5*, 227–229. Available from https://doi.org/10.1037/per0000008.

Vernon, P. A., Villani, V. C., Vickers, L. C., & Harris, J. A. (2008). A behavioral genetic investigation of the dark triad and the big 5. *Personality and Individual Differences, 44*, 445–452. Available from https://doi.org/10.1016/j.paid.2007.09.007.

Vogel, E., Rose, J. P., Roberts, L., & Eckles, K. (2014). Social comparison, social media, and self-esteem. *Psychology of Popular Media Culture, 3*, 206–222. Available from https://doi.org/10.1037/ppm0000047.

Wang, D. (2017). A study of the relationship between narcissism, extraversion, drive for entertainment, and narcissistic behavior on social networking sites. *Computers in Human Behavior, 66*, 138–146. Available from https://doi.org/10.1016/j.chb.2016.09.036.

Weiser, E. (2015). #Me: Narcissism and its facets as predictors of selfie-posting frequency a study of the relationship between narcissism, extraversion, drive for entertainment, and narcissistic behavior on social networking sites. *Personality and Individual Differences, 86*, 477–481. Available from https://doi.org/10.1016/j.paid.2015.07.007.

Wink, P. (1991). Two faces of narcissism. *Journal of Personality and Social Psychology, 61*, 590–597. Available from https://doi.org/10.1037/0022-3514.61.

Winter, S., Neubaum, G., Eimler, S. C., Gordon, V., Theil, J., Herrmann, J., et al. (2014). Another brick in the facebook wall—how personality traits relate to the content of status updates. *Computers in Human Behavior, 34*, 194–202. Available from https://doi.org/10.1016/j.chb.2014.01.048.

Cyberstalking and Bullying

Cyberstalking and bullying reveal the dark side of social media in terms of exploitation. Cyberstalking is a serious predatory behavior and reflective of the innate, human tendency to control and intimidate others. In terms of evolutionary psychology, it has been around eons of time for predatory survival and control. It can be argued that bullying reflects a class of natural, adaptive behaviors that result in the bully acquiring more access to resources and reputation. For your ancestors, this helped with survival and mating. Research reveals that contrary to cultural beliefs, some people don't bully others because they lack social skills or have low self-esteem (Volk, Dane, Marini, & Vaillancourt, 2015). Rather, bullies may be in relatively better condition than their targets, with bullies displaying similar or better mental and physical health. In addition, they may have improved social and leadership skills, setting the stage for the prospect of greater mating success. Volk et al. (2015) reported a positive relationship between bullying and engaging in dating and sexual relationships controlling for age, sex, reported victimization, attractiveness, and likability. Bullying emerged as a positive predictor for the number of dating partners and sexual encounters. Bullies tended to have a greater number of sexual partners, though this effect was modest. Conversely, being a victim of bullying did not affect the number of sexual partners one had while it was positively correlated the number of dating partners. This might reflect the evolutionary possibility that other same-sex individuals might view those who seek to date frequently, as competitors, and bullied in order to prevent such behavior from taking place.

This chapter defines types of stalking and notes similarities and differences between face-to-face stalking and electronic stalking. Characteristics of cyberstalkers are presented as well as cyberbullying. Cyberbullying among children and college students is discussed. Sex differences are briefly reviewed in terms of the targets of bullying. The use of mental imagery in the form of imagined interactions (IIs) is apparent in cyberstalking, and individuals may imagine that outcome of their predatory tactics. What is teasing to someone, is bullying to another. There is a discussion on the ramifications of FINSTAS and RINSTAS. The chapter concludes with a brief discussion of the availability of phone apps to deal with bullying.

The United Kingdom established the National Centre for Cyberstalking Research at the University of Bedfordshire to analyze the motivation and characteristics of cyberstalkers, which is a recurring problem (see https://www.beds.ac.uk/research-ref/irac/nccr). The American equivalent is broader and includes concerns with national defense and cyberterrorism. The National Cyber Security Alliance, which is the American equivalent, is a nonprofit agency founded in 2001. The alliance has affiliations with the US Department of Homeland Security including Comcast, Facebook, Google, Microsoft, PayPal, and Symantec (see https://en.wikipedia.org/wiki/National_Cyber_Security_Alliance).

According to Spitzberg and Hoobler (2002), the social scientific analysis did not begin until the 1990s. Before we discuss cyberstalking, we will briefly discuss the more general term of stalking. Originally, stalking involved behavioral invasion and referred to nonelectronic means of intrusion (e.g., physical surveillance, mailing letters). Stalking is related to a phenomenon referred to as obsessive relational intrusion (ORI), which is designed for intimacy development (Cupach & Spitzberg, 2000, 2004; Spitzberg, 2001). ORI is an unwanted desire for intimacy through repetitive invasion of a person's sense of physical or symbolic privacy. Famous cases of this are groupies stalking celebrities. This has become as CWS or celebrity worship syndrome (McCutcheon, Lange, & Houran, 2002). Famous cases include former talk show host, David Letterman who was stalked for 5 years by a woman who claimed to be his wife when she had no personal connection to him. Other celebrities who have fallen victim to this form of stalking include Jennifer Aniston, Halle Berry, Jodie Foster, and Mila Kunis to name just a few.

Social media can encourage CWS because of the proliferation of news and gossip about media figures. Indeed, media and advertising is strategically designed to expose consumers to manipulated images and expectations designed to trigger brain neurotransmitters for pleasure. Furthermore, social media encourages CWS because it sells more products and has more viewers and followers. Cyberstalking of celebrities has resulted in prison sentences. There was the famous case of Christopher Haney who hacked into the accounts of Scarlett Johansson, Christina Aguilera, Miley Cyrus, Jessica Alba, Selena Gomez, and Demi Lovato (Girard, 2013). He sold nude photos to online gossip sites as well as retrieving business contracts and contact lists, which allowed him to find other celebrity victims.

Most stalking is a form of ORI, but the two phenomena are not isomorphic. Some stalking is purely for the sake of terrorism or destruction, as with political or underworld assassinations. Conversely, ORI does not have to be threatening, as in a socially unskilled paramour simply annoying or pestering an object of affection. Despite these differences, research shows that even relatively mild efforts at such courtship often cross the threshold of threat and fear by virtue of their repetition, inappropriateness, timing, and/or oddity (Cupach & Spitzberg, 2000; Sinclair & Frieze, 2000).

DEFINITIONS OF CYBERSTALKING

In its most basic form, cyberstalking represents a motivational state in which social media platforms are used to intimidate one or more individuals through surveillance. There are various definitions due to the burgeoning technologies that have arisen in the 21st century. Bocij and McFarlane (2002) offer the following definition:

> A group of behaviors in which an individual, group of individuals or organization, uses information and communications technology to harass another individual, group of individuals or organization. Such behaviors may include, but are not limited to, the transmission of threats and false accusations, damage to data or

equipment, identity theft, data theft, computer monitoring, the solicitation of minors for sexual purposes and any form of aggression. Harassment is defined as a course of action that a reasonable person, in possession of the same information, would think causes another reasonable person to suffer emotional distress (p. 32).

Spitzberg and Hoobler (2002) provide four criteria for defining cyberstalking. First, there is a repetitive course of conduct. Second, there is an invasion of the target's personal privacy. Third, there must be evidence of threat regarding justice and adjudication. Spitzberg and Hoobler (2002) discuss how frequent phone calls or emails are unlikely to reflect stalking "unless the content, form, or nature of those communications are sufficient to elicit fear or a sense of dread from any 'reasonable person'" (p. 69). Fourth, stalking can occur if a threat is made to the target concerning members of their social network including family, friends, pets, or property. Hence, there is persistent, unwanted online monitoring or contact with a target to the point of obsession. The electronic devices do not limit geographic or temporal separation. Cyberstalkers are frequently expartners. Next, we briefly discuss cyberbullying.

SIMILARITIES AND DIFFERENCES BETWEEN FACE-TO-FACE AND CYBERBULLYING

Face-to-face bullying and cyberbullying are similar in various ways. Obviously, both involve aggression designed to harm or ridicule a target. According to the Gale Student Resources in Context (2016) website, both types of bullies are interested in inflicting pain. Both types occur again and again.

Both types of bullying involve a power imbalance in which the balance of power supports the bully. Bullies tend to target passive targets who are unlikely or unable to defend themselves with less fear of reprisal. The targets of both types of bulling are often emotionally devastated by this harassment. Numerous studies have shown that they frequently suffer from depression, social discomfort, low self-esteem, or similar complaints (e.g., Honeycutt & Sheldon, 2018; Kowalski, Giumetti, Schroeder, & Lattanner, 2014). Table 3.1 highlights the differences between face-to-face bullying and cyberbullying.

Cyberbullying can occur through a short message service on mobile devices, text, apps, or online in social media, forums, and gaming where people can view, participate in, or share content. It includes sending, posting, or sharing negative, harmful, false, or malicious content about

TABLE 3.1 Differences From Cyber and Face-to-Face Bullying

1. Anonymity can be established through pseudo identities, or different media accounts
2. Scope of Cyberbullying is larger—Cyberbullies can create posts online defaming their victims whenever they choose. Traditional bullying occurs in a more restricted, physical area
3. Due to online posting, the targets are emotionally harassed in front of larger audiences
4. Learned helplessness by cyberbullying victims—Due to the uninhibited nature of cyberbullies, victims of online abuse may fear reprisal more than the victims of traditional bullies
5. Perpetual effect of cyberbullying—While some face-to-face bulling involves two or more bullies harassing a target, online viewers can play a role in perpetuating the actions of a cyberbully through forwarding or sharing hurtful messages

Adapted from http://ic.galegroup.com/ic/suic/ReferenceDetailsPage/DocumentToolsPortletWindow? displayGroupName = Reference&u = groves&p = SUIC&action = 2&catId = &documentId = GALE% 7CEJ2181500310&zid = 6fd20aaf5793389959fde88575ac3810.

someone else. Cyberbullying is direct when texts are sent directly to the target. However, once that occurs, the target is likely to block the bullies' messages unless they have been directed by legal officials to keep a cybertrail. Indeed, cyberbullying can become a crime if you do any of the following:

- Make violent threats
- Make death threats
- Make obscene and harassing phone calls and texts
- Sexting
- Sextortion that is sexual exploitation
- Child pornography
- Express hate crimes
- Post and take a photo of someone in a place where they expect privacy

According to the Cyberbullying Research Center, 44 American states have anticyberbullying laws with the exceptions of Minnesota, Wyoming, Nebraska, New Mexico, New Hampshire, and Maine (https://cyberbullying.org/bullying-laws). Currently, there is no federal law, policy, or school sanction against cyberbullying. States vary in if it's a school policy or off-campus sanction. The sanctions range from school suspension to jail time. While Montana has a criminal law, it is the only state with no school sanction. International law deals with cybercrime in the treaty signed by the Council of Europe at the Budapest Convention on Cybercrime (2001). While it deals with racism and xenophobia, it does not mention cyberbullying.

Research on cyberbullying is common among children. For example, Raskauskas and Stoltz (2007) found that targets of face-to-face bullying were likely to have received cyberbullying. It has been found that 75 of 284 (26%) traditional victims were also victims of cyberbullying and 42 (15%) victims of traditional bullying perpetrated cyberbullying (Smith et al., 2008). Students in their study believed that bullying through the use of a picture/video clip or in a chat room would have a greater effect than face-to-face bullying. Ybarra, Diener-West, and Leaf (2007) found that 36% of youth aged 10–15 who were harassed online also reported being bullied at school. This bullying was associated with high anxiety and drug/alcohol use. In addition, those who had experienced online harassment had increased behavior problems and weapon-carrying at school.

CYBERBULLYING AMONG COLLEGE STUDENTS

Cyberbullying among college students reveals that 46.1% of the targets reported text messaging as the most frequent medium for cyberbullying, followed by 43.5% reporting email, and 36.2% web-sites (Zalaquett & Chatters, 2014). Also, 44% of the students cyber-bullied in college reported being bullied by a fellow student, 42% reported being cyberbullied by friends, 22.6% by a boyfriend or girl-friend, 22.6% by someone unknown to them, and 5.3% reported being cyberbullied by a coworker. However, over 40% of the cyber-bullied college students reported multiple role relations with the bully.

An interesting, but significant finding was that Asian-Americans experienced cyberbullying more frequently than African-American, Hispanic American, or European-Americans. Research conducted among high school populations have found cyberbullying to be more prevalent among multiethnic populations and to have a significant impact on the well-being and self-esteem of Asian-American and Pacific Islander youth (Goebert, Else, Matsu, Chung-Do, & Chang, 2011). Hence, there may be elements of racism and prejudice, which reflect out-group stereotyping (Mulvey, Hitti, & Killen, 2010; Raabe & Beelmann, 2011).

Zalaquett and Chatters (2014) report a statistically significant associa-tion between cyberbullying in high school and its occurrence in college with approximately 35% of the targets of cyberbullying in college experiencing it in high school, which accounted for approximately 15% of the total sample of 613 students. In terms of emotion and stress, approximately 45% of the targets reported feeling angry, 41% felt sad, 32% reported experiencing an increase in stress, and 9% reported experiencing a loss of productivity. Only 6% reported experiencing no effects. Finally, 77% of the sample favored education on cyberbullying, which indicates participants feel that there is a need for more education on this type of bullying. In addition, approximately 38.5% ($n = 235$) of participants indicated they had given their phone number to someone unknown over the Internet, which denotes a need for more education regarding Internet safety. Incidentally, a common way that this information is innocently disseminated is through the use of electronic signatures containing contact information (e.g., name, position, email, and phone number).

SEX DIFFERENCES

Kowalski and Limber (2013) found sex differences in cyberbullying. They reported that for males who bullied others, anxiety and depression scores closely paralleled levels of males not involved with bullying. This applied whether the bullying was electronic or face to face. For females who bullied the rates of anxiety and depression were higher when compared with females who were not involved with face-to-face or electronic bullying. Another research reveals that females were more likely than males to post gossip about others to hurt them (Marcum, Higgins, Freiburger, & Ricketts, 2012). This finding confirms previous literature that asserted females participate in bullying that involves emotional and psychological abuse, which involves gossiping and spreading of information (whether true or untrue) (Owens, Shute, & Slee, 2000; Underwood, Galen, & Paquette, 2001). Relatedly, Volk et al. (2015) found that women who bullied had higher dating interests and partners compared to men. Hence, degradation of competing partners serves an important evolutionary function.

Females prefer participating in behavior that is not physically confrontational, and by hiding behind the protection of an electronic forum, they can be more brazen with their behavior (Marcum et al., 2012). It is interesting that in areas torn apart by war and divided cultures, cyberbullying takes place as a way to ostracize outgroup members. For example, during the Northern Ireland and United Kingdom conflict, men were more likely to be bullied in face-to-face encounters, while young women reported higher levels of cyberbullying (Savoldi, de Abreu, & Alavares, 2016). Social media sites allowed another avenue for bullies (no pun intended) in Belfast, a divided city to increase verbal ridicule. The anonymity of the web allows bullies to remain anonymous and avoid immediate physical confrontation. Bullying took the form of harassment, threats of violence, sectarianism and vulgar messages with much online bullying seemingly a continuation of offline behaviors. And while young men were more likely to be the victims of bullying in the real world, young women reported higher levels of cyberbullying.

Future research is warranted, which examines sex differences not only in the frequency of experiencing cyberbullying but also in reactions to it. Research is also needed looking at males' and females' involvement in cyberbullying via different venues. Because of our interest in comparing electronic bullying with traditional bullying, we used overall prevalence rates of involvement in cyberbullying. It may be, however, that males are more likely to be involved in and more likely to be affected by particular types of cyberbullying (e.g., video gaming) than females.

Flaming. Flaming occurs when the target is harassed in public forums, such as Facebook, or a virtual chat group, as opposed to private emails or texting. Hence, cyberbullies don't send malicious messages to victims directly but within the chat group so others can see. Flaming through shaming is designed to make the target lose some of their credibility or reputation within the group, and through this ostracism may result in the target feeling like they cannot be part of the group and become an outcast. The idea behind flaming is to start an "emotional fire" in the target by initial posts with the intent that the ridicule and repercussion intensify and spread. Betraying confidence is a type of cyberbullying and occurs when the personal disclosure of another is spread through a social network, which embarrasses the target. It is one of the most popular ways to terminate friendships and create uncertainty in interpersonal relationships (Honeycutt & Sheldon, 2018). It is often done through satirical posts as a type of aggressive teasing. Aggressive teasing is discussed next in terms of mental imagery through the use of IIs.

IMAGINED INTERACTIONS, CYBER TEASING, AND BULLYING

Cyberbullying can be premediated as well as an instantaneous reaction to posting in which the bully may not like a given message and retaliates with aggressive messages. Premediated cyberbullying means that the bully is likely to use IIs, which is a form of social cognition, imagery, and daydreaming in which people mentally plan what they are going to say (Honeycutt, 2003, 2015). A series of studies have revealed that teasers and bullies, sometimes, plan their bullying episode. A major function of IIs is rehearsal. Hence, bullies can plan what they are going to post and anticipate the reactions to it. Valence refers to the amount and diversity of emotions that are experienced while having an II (Honeycutt, 2015). While envisioning teasing, it is possible for positive, negative, or mixed emotions to occur. Therefore those who plan aggressive teasing may enjoy it in terms of the German notion of "schadenfreude" in which people take pleasure at the grief or ridicule of others.

Honeycutt and Wright (2017) examined affectionate and aggressive teasing. Affectionate teasing is a playful form of positive communication that reflects socially appropriate uses of humor to enhance interpersonal bonds. The high level of humor and a moderate level of identity confrontation in affectionate teasing help to minimize the ambiguity regarding the intent of the provocation. Common examples of playful teasing on Facebook are posting pictures of friends who are doing something fun but with a twist (for example, showing friend falling in the water skiing while attempting to use one ski). Recently, the third author's wife posted about him cooking a meal for her after she seriously damaged her hand in an accident and he took over as a "gourmet" with little experience.

Aggressive teasing is cruel and moderate in humor and ambiguity, and high in identity confrontation (Kowalski et al., 2001). Aggressive teasing is designed to denigrate the identity of the target and create relational distance, and social rejection. This signals a deliberate effort to invoke face threat rather than playful jest as aggressive teasing is employed for destructive ends (Kowalski, 2007).

A major function of IIs is conflict-linkage in which people deal with arguments and grievances introspectively. It is possible that ruminating about arguments is associated with vindictive cyber teasing as catharsis is released while keeping the prior conflicts alive. Indeed, recall the notion of gunny sacking in which people unleash repressed grievances from the past, which may be unrelated to the current argument (see Honeycutt & Sheldon, 2018). Honeycutt and Wright (2017) found that self-esteem was positively associated with affectionate teasing and negatively related to aggressive teasing. Aggressive teasing was characterized by using IIs to ruminate about conflict, catharsis, and rehearsal.

While teasing can be friendly or negative, bullying is a blatant act of aggression in which the goal is to harm the survivor (Juvonen & Graham, 2014). Research reveals that bullies have IIs with a target following the encounter (Krawietz & Honeycutt, 2017). In addition, these

IIs elicit positive emotions. Hence, the cyber bully enjoys replaying the posts. They may use visual imagery in which they fantasize about how the target may be agonizing over the post or video. Verbal imagery is used in terms of posting content of the message while mixed imagery represents a combination of both (Honeycutt, 2003).

As for the finding of retroactivity and positive valence, bullies could possibly be thought of as basking in their glory in accordance with game theory, which explains conflict and cooperation and is based on strategic foresight. Game theory investigates interactions between individuals in which they make decisions that could affect one parties in the interaction (Bostrom, 1970; Honeycutt & Eldredge, 2015; Rasmusen, 2007; Von Neumann & Morgenstern, 1953). When cyberbullying is viewed as a power, dominance game, trigger strategies can be used in terms of game theory based on successive iterations of moves (episodes) (Mailath & Samuelson, 2006). Relatedly, Macklem (2003) discusses how children who are both bullies and targets, fight back which excites the bully and lose when confronted by an aggressive bully. Research reveals that a small group of individuals that are regularly bullied also bully others (Kowalski & Limber, 2013). Relatedly, general strain theory espouses that the strain and stress of bullying can have disastrous, long-term outcomes in terms of deviancy (Agnew, 2006). There may be a cycle of bullying-target-antisocial behavioral reaction. The antisocial behaviors are due to finding an outlet for emotions. Unfortunately, in this cycle, the antisocial behaviors resemble the II catharsis function that is dysfunctional. Research confirms that both bullies and targets are often emotionally harmed by cyberbullying.

Targets of bullying can use retroactive and proactive IIs to predict how the bully will respond. One reason for the positively affected retroactive IIs for bullies may be because they have reached an outcome or payoff that benefits them the best. One speculation for satisfaction comes from research conducted by Berger and Caravita (2015) in which they discovered that Machiavellianism and perceived popularity are associated with the bully. So, based on their finding, we speculate that individuals who bully could forecast or replay encounters in their head determine how successful their manipulative tactics were. If these tactics were in fact successful, then the end result could be positive IIs.

An interesting mechanism for bullies and targets is to set up multiple social media accounts to hide their identity and only make it available to selected friends. FINSTAs stand for fake Instagram accounts. Conversely, RINSTAs are real Instagram accounts. While these are often used to prevent employer oversight, RINSTAs are associated with a user's first and surname. The RINSTA account is likely the one that is

TABLE 3.2   Characteristics of Fake and Real Instagram Account Users

- Dominated by female, teenage users (though boys use them too)
- Finsta handles are often sexually explicit
- Finsta handles are elusive in order to escape the detection of searches by employers, parents, or schools, but obvious enough to be known by their friends
- A Finsta's creator can be traced by an experienced user by analyzing the Finsta's followers, posts, and respective reactions and interactions with other users, such as likes, comments, and regrams (reposting for other users to view)
- Finstas often intentionally cross paths with Rinstas (real Instagrams) to launch social media cyberbullying and emotional abuse
- Due to their anonymity, Finstas are a preferred platform for teens to strategically humiliate, ostracize, and bully others
- Although Finstas may begin with good intentions, most ultimately digress into a conduit for cyber aggression or fan the flames of social drama in the form of likes, comments, and regrams
- Finstas that create mental, psychological, or emotional trauma are subject to school-related discipline if and when they eventually bleed into and disrupt the learning environment of school. The lines of outside bullying and school have become increasingly blurred by social media platforms

Adapted from https://www.huffingtonpost.com/entry/what-the-finsta-the-darker-world-of-teenagers-and_us_57eb9e03e4b07f20daa0fefb.

revealed in a Google search. The FINSTAs usually have a fictional screen name that is based on an inside joke or some identifying characteristic that only that person's close friends know about. Table 3.2 reveals various characteristics of FINSTAs and RINSTAs. The following quote is poignant in terms of cyberbullying is easily facilitated by FINSTAs.

FINSTAs have become the Wild West of social media: the only rule is that there are no rules; couple that with (perceived) anonymity, angst, sexual curiosity, envy, insecurity, relationships and rivalry, etc. and you have entered the world of FINSTAs. The world of FINSTAs is fun, until it isn't; users are anonymous, until they aren't; they're harmless, until they're malicious, and they have no impact, until their blunt force trauma takes teens out at the knees (Patterson, 2016).

PHONE APPS TO DEAL WITH BULLYING

There are numerous phone apps that provide information and coping links to deal with bullying (e.g., KnowBullying, STOP!T, BullyButton, BullyTag). The third author who is the senior managing editor of the journal, *Imagination, Cognition, and Personality* has received various invitations to advertise some of these apps. While there are daily challenges that cultures face when keeping youth safe, it is important that life skills be taught to children for them better understand the precarious dangers of the internet. The cyber safety phone app views this uncertainty as an opportunity to engage teachers and parents and implement technology to teach children how to navigate these challenges. UpGo (https://www.4upgo.com/) teaches kids how to

- address cyberbullying, sexting, privacy and online predators;
- manage strong emotions and handle new, tough situations;
- make thoughtful decisions; and
- ask for help, and from whom, without fear and intimidation.

Another digital organization called, "I Witness Bullying" created an EMOJI, phone app to help bystanders report bullying instances (see http://iwitnessbullying.org/?gclid = EAIaIQobChMIm8yEy9HL2gIVj YbACh3RMwLmEAAYASAAEgIR4PD_BwE). They provide phone numbers including 911 to call when someone is being bullied, whether it is cyber or face-to-face bullying. The Pacer Portal is a link sponsored by the National (American) Bullying Prevention Center that provides prevention links, educational and awareness toolkits, contest ideas, and promotional materials.

The Trevor Support Center is a place where Lesbian, Gay, Bi, Transexual, Queer (LGBTQ) youth can find information to answer to frequently asked questions and explore resources related to bullying about sexual orientation and gender identity. The Bully Project Mural is a digital site where people can share art, stories, and perspectives about bullying, its impact, and how the community can help stop it. In addition, there is a link that encourages taking action instead of mere observation that is called "Ten Ways To Be An Upstander: Tips and tools for ways to help stop bullying."

CONCLUSION AND IMPLICATIONS

Cyberstalking and bullying represent the dark side of human nature in a technological age. From an evolutionary viewpoint, bullying is done to denigrate potential mating rivals. This is similar to the evolutionary function of cognitive jealousy, in which people believe that they may have competing rivals. Bullying has existed to demonstrate power since the dawn of times. Hence, electronic media is merely often a convenient mechanism to continue the enduring behavior, while offering some degree of anonymity if desired as well as not being in the physical presence of the target.

There is a wide body of research based on social learning theory in which many people are both in the role of bullies and targets. Bullying and the extension to cyberbullying is a learned behavior (Swearer, Wang, Berry, & Myers, 2014). For example, children who are exposed to domestic violence in their homes are significantly more likely to bully others than those who are not exposed to domestic violence (Baldry, 2003; Bowes et al., 2009). In addition, the transference principle of psychotherapy fits in nicely with cyberbullying. Transference is subconscious act of transferring feelings and attitudes associated with one's past experiences to someone (e.g., a new target) or something in the present.

Legal remedies to cyberbullying have been used as earlier noted. It is typical for cyberbullying sites to provide intuitive list of what to do (e.g., protecting your password, censoring photos, and setting up privacy controls). It is interesting that the "golden rule" is stated as rule number 10 by the Cyberbullying Research Center (Hinduja & Patchin, 2012). They state, "Don't be a cyberbully yourself. Treat others how you would want to be treated. By being a jerk to others online, you are reinforcing the idea that the behavior is acceptable." Finally, there are various phone apps that are easily googled to empower people to deal with bullying. Indeed, pictures are easily taken of bullying incidents, which can facilitate deterrence.

References

Agnew, R. (2006). *Pressured into crime: An overview of general strain theory.* New York: Oxford University Press.

Baldry, A. C. (2003). Bullying in schools and exposure to domestic violence. *Child Abuse & Neglect, 27,* 713–732. Available from https://doi.org/10.1016/S0145-2134(03)00114-5.

Berger, C., & Caravita, S. C. S. (2015). Why do early adolescents bully? Exploring the influence of preside norms on social and psychological motives. *Journal of Adolescence, 46,* 45–46. Available from https://doi.org/10.1016/j.adolescence.2015.10.020.

Bocij, P., & McFarlane, L. (2002). Online harassment: Towards a definition of cyberstalking. *Prison Service Journal, 39,* 31–38.

Bostrom, R. N. (1970). Rejoinder: Games and communication purpose. *Journal of Communication, 20,* 121–124. Available from https://doi.org/10.1111/j.1460-2466.1970.tb00869.

Bowes, L., Arseneault, L., Maughan, B., Taylor, A., Caspi, A., & Moffitt, T. E. (2009). School, neighborhood, and family factors are associated with children's bullying involvement: A nationally representative longitudinal study. *Journal of the American Academy of Child Adolescent Psychiatry, 48,* 545–553. Available from https://doi.org/10.1097/CHI.0b013e31819cb017.

Convention on Cybercrime. (2001, November 23). *Budapest*. Retrieved March 2, 2018 from <https://www.coe.int/en/web/conventions/full-list/-/conventions/treaty/185>.

Cupach, W., & Spitzberg, B. (2000). Obsessive relational intrusion: Incidence, perceived severity, and coping. *Violence and Victims, 15*, 357–372. Available from https://doi.org/10.4135/9781412958479.n380.

Cupach, W., & Spitzberg, B. (2004). *The dark side of relational pursuit: From attraction to obsession and stalking*. Mahwah, NJ: Erlbaum.

Gale Student Resources in Context. (2016). *Differences between cyberbullying and traditional bullying*. Gale: Student Resources in Context. <http://link.galegroup.com/apps/doc/EJ2181500310/SUIC?u = groves&xid = 5784611d> Accessed 24.02.18.

Girard, K. (2013). Scarlett Johansson Hacker Christoper Haney: Does punishment fit crime? *The Improper Magazine*. Retrieved from https://www.theimproper.com/51420/scarlett-johansson-hacker-christoper-haney-does-punishment-fit-crime/.

Goebert, D., Else, I., Matsu, C., Chung-Do, J., & Chang, J. Y. (2011). The impact of cyberbullying on substance abuse and mental health in a multiethnic sample. *Maternal and Child Health Journal, 15*, 1282–1286. Available from https://doi.org/10.1007/s10995-0100672-x.

Hinduja, S., & Patchin, J.W. (2012). *Preventing cyberbullying: Top ten tips for teens*. Retrieved from <https://cyberbullying.org/Top-Ten-Tips-Teens-Prevention.pdf>.

Honeycutt, J. M. (2003). *Imagined interactions: Daydreaming about communication*. Cresskill, NJ: Hampton.

Honeycutt, J. M. (2015). Imagined interaction theory: Mental representations of interpersonal communication. In D. O. Braithwaite, & P. Schrodt (Eds.), *Engaging theories in interpersonal communication* (2nd ed., pp. 75–87). Thousand Oaks, CA: Sage.

Honeycutt, J. M., & Eldredge, J. H. (2015). Applying game theory and signal detection theory to conflict escalation: A case study of a police investigator viewing a domestic argument. In K. Chapman (Ed.), *Decision and game theory: Perspectives, applications and challenges* (pp. 17–30). New York, NY: Nova Science.

Honeycutt, J. M., & Sheldon, P. A. (2018). *Scripts and communication for relationships* (2nd ed.). New York: Peter Lang.

Honeycutt, J. M., & Wright, C. N. (2017). Predicting affectionate and aggressive teasing motivation on the basis of self-esteem and imagined interactions with the victim. *Southern Communication Journal, 82*, 15–26. Available from https://doi.org/10.1080/1041794X.2016.1265577.

Juvonen, J., & Graham, S. (2014). Bullying in schools: The power of bullies and the plight of victims. *Annual Review of Psychology, 65*, 159–185. Available from https://doi.org/10.1146/annurev-psych-010213-115030.

Kowalski, R. M. (2007). Teasing and bullying. In B. H. Spitzberg, & W. R. Cupach (Eds.), *The dark side of interpersonal communication* (pp. 169–197). Mahwah, NJ: Lawrence Erlbaum.

Kowalski, R. M., Howerton, E., & McKenzie, M. (2001). Permitted disrespect: Teasing in interpersonal interactions. In R. M. Kowalski (Ed.), *Behaving badly: Aversive behaviors in interpersonal relationships* (pp. 177–202). Washington DC: American Psychological Association, 2001.

Kowalski, R. M., Giumetti, G. W., Schroeder, A. N., & Lattanner, M. R. (2014). Bullying in the digital age: A critical review and meta-analysis of cyberbullying research among youth. *Psychological Bulletin, 140*(4), 1073–1137. Available from https://doi.org/10.1037/a0035618.

Kowalski, R. M., & Limber, S. P. (2013). Psychological, physical, and academic correlates of cyberbullying and traditional bullying. *Journal of Adolescent Health, 53*, 513–520. Available from https://doi.org/10.1016/j.jadohealth.2012.09.018.

Krawietz, C.E., & Honeycutt, J.M. (2017, November). An investigation of bullying perpetrators and victims' usage of imagined interactions. In *Paper presented at the annual national communication association conference*, Dallas, TX.

Macklem, G. L. (2003). *Bullying and teasing: Social power in children's groups*. New York: Springer.

Mailath, G., & Samuelson, L. (2006). *Repeated games and reputations: Long-run relationships*. New York: Oxford University Press.

Marcum, C. D., Higgins, G. E., Freiburger, T. L., & Ricketts, M. L. (2012). Battle of the sexes: An examination of male and female cyber bullying. *International Journal of Cyber Criminology*, 6, 904−911. Available from http://www.cybercrimejournal.com/marcumetal2012janijcc.pdf.

McCutcheon, L. E., Lange, R., & Houran, J. (2002). Conceptualization and measurement of celebrity worship. *British Journal of Psychology*, 93, 67−87. Available from https://doi.org/10.1348/000712602162454.

Mulvey, K. L., Hitti, A., & Killen, M. (2010). The development of stereotyping and exclusion. *Wiley Interdisciplinary Reviews: Cognitive Science*, 1(4), 597−606. Available from https://doi.org/10.1002/wcs.66.

Owens, L., Shute, R., & Slee, P. (2000). Guess what I just heard! Indirect aggression among teenage girls in Australia. *Aggressive Behavior*, 26, 67−83. Available from https://doi.org/10.1002/(SICI)1098-2337(2000)26:1%3C67::AID-AB6%3E3.0.CO;2-C.

Patterson, D. (2016). *What the Finsta?! The Darker World of Teenagers and Instagram*. Retrieved March 31, 2018 from <https://www.huffingtonpost.com/entry/what-the-finsta-the-darker-world-of-teenagers-and_us_57eb9e03e4b07f20daa0fefb>.

Raabe, T., & Beelmann, A. (2011). Development of ethnic, racial, and national prejudice in childhood and adolescence: A multinational meta-analysis of age differences. *Child Development*, 82(6), 1715−1737. Available from https://doi.org/10.1111/j.1467-8624.2011.01668.x.

Raskauskas, J., & Stoltz, A. (2007). Involvement in traditional and electronic bullying among adolescents. *Developmental Psychology*, 43, 564−575. Available from https://doi.org/10.1037/0012-1649.43.3.564.

Rasmusen, E. (2007). *Games and information: An introduction to game theory* (4th ed.). Malden, MA: Blackwell Publishing.

Savoldi, S., de Abreu, P. F., & Alavares, C. (2016). Bullying, cyberbullying and internet usage among young people in post-conflict Belfast. *Cogent Social Sciences*, 2(1), 1132985. Available from https://doi.org/10.1080/23311886.2015.1132985.

Sinclair, H., & Frieze, I. (2000). Initial courtship behavior and stalking: How should we draw the line? *Violence and Victims*, 15, 23−40.

Smith, P. K., Mahdavi, J., Carvalho, M., Fisher, S., Shanette, R., & Tippett, N. (2008). Cyberbullying: Its nature and impact in secondary school pupils. *Journal of Child Psychology and Psychiatry*, 49, 376−385. Available from https://doi.org/10.1111/j.1469-7610.2007.01846.x.

Spitzberg, B. (2001). Obsessive relational intrusion, coping, and sexual coercion victimization. *Communication Reports*, 14, 19−31. Available from https://doi.org/10.1080/0893421010936773.

Spitzberg, B. H., & Hoobler, G. (2002). Cyberstalking and the technologies of interpersonal terrorism. *New Media & Society*, 71−92. Available from https://doi.org/10.1177/14614440222226271.

Swearer, S. M., Wang, C., Berry, B., & Myers, Z. R. (2014). Reducing bullying: Application of social cognitive theory. *Theory into Practice*, 53, 271−277. Available from https://doi.org/10.1080/00405841.2014.947221.

Underwood, M., Galen, B., & Paquette, J. (2001). Top ten challenges for understanding gender and aggression in children: Why can't we all just get along? *Social Development*, *10*, 248–266. Available from https://doi.org/10.1111/1467-9507.00162.

Volk, A., Dane, A., Marini, Z., & Vaillancourt, T. (2015). Adolescent bullying, dating, and mating: Testing an evolutionary hypothesis. *Evolutionary Psychology*. Available from https://doi.org/10.1177/1474704915613909.

Von Neumann, J., & Morgenstern, O. (1953). *Theory of games and economic behavior* (3rd ed.). Princeton, NJ: Princeton University Press.

Ybarra, M. L., Diener-West, M., & Leaf, P. J. (2007). *Journal of Adolescent Health*, *4*, 2–50. Available from https://doi.org/10.1016/j.jadohealth.2007.09.004.

Zalaquett, C. P., & Chatters, S. J. (2014). Cyberbullying in college: Frequency, characteristics, and practical implications. *Sage Open*, 1–8. Available from https://doi.org/10.1177/2158244014526721.

CHAPTER

4

Negative Social Comparisons on Social Network Sites

SOCIAL COMPARISON THEORY

As earlier mentioned, *social comparison theory* (Festinger, 1954) posits that individuals have a natural drive to compare their own attributes and abilities with the abilities and attributes of others. Festinger based his theory on nine hypotheses (see Table 4.1)— explaining why people engage in social comparisons, with whom they will compare, and some of the consequences of social comparisons to the self. According to Festinger (1954), the need to know the self, combined with the impossibility of determining the abilities of

TABLE 4.1   Hypotheses of the Theory of Social Comparison Processes

No.	Hypotheses
I	There exists, in the human organism, a drive to evaluate his opinions and his abilities
II	To the extent that objective, nonsocial means are not available, people evaluate their opinions and abilities by comparison respectively with the opinions and abilities of others
III	The tendency to compare oneself with some other specific person decreases as the difference between his opinion or ability and one's own increases
IV	There is a unidirectional drive upward in the case of abilities, which is largely absent in opinions
V	There are nonsocial restraints that make it difficult or even impossible to change one's ability. These nonsocial restraints are largely absent for opinions
VI	The cessation of comparison with others is accompanied by hostility or derogation to the extent that continued comparison with those persons implies unpleasant consequences
VII	Any factors that increase the importance of some particular group as a comparison group for some particular opinion or ability will increase the pressure toward uniformity concerning that ability or opinion within that group
VIII	If persons who are very divergent from one's own opinion or ability are perceived as different from oneself on attributes consistent with the divergence, the tendency to narrow the range of comparability becomes stronger
IX	When there is a range of opinion or ability in a group, the relative strength of the three manifestations of pressures toward uniformity will be different for those who are close to the mode of the group than those who are distant from the mode. Specifically, those close to the mode of the group will have stronger tendencies to change the positions of others, relatively weaker tendencies to narrow the range of comparison, and much weaker tendencies to change their position compared to those who are distant from the mode of the group

From Festinger, L. (1954). A theory of social comparison processes. Human Relations, 7, 117–140.

others, motivates people to compare themselves to other people. People tend to seek out similar others for comparisons—or in the case of abilities, others who are slightly better on related attributes. The need to self-improve is therefore another reason for social comparisons (Taylor & Lobel, 1989). Most of the time people do not compare themselves with dissimilar others, as the result of this comparison would remain ambiguous.

Social comparison theory has been used to explain different phenomena in applied contexts. For example, researchers have studied the importance of comparisons with others in academic performance (e.g., Marsh & Hau, 2003; Marsh & Parker, 1984), decision-making in organizations (Bandura & Jourden, 1991), romantic relationships and marital functioning (e.g., Buunk, VanYperen, Taylor, & Collins, 1991; Lockwood, Dolderrnan, Sadler, & Gerchak, 2004), gossip (Wert & Salovey, 2004), and body image processes (Sheldon, 2010). Most research has focused on appearance-related comparisons and the role of media in evaluating one's attractiveness.

MASS MEDIA AND SOCIAL COMPARISONS

Media play an important role in establishing cultural standards of beauty. Currently, in the western world, being beautiful means being thin. This is especially problematic for women as they are judged by their physical appearance. Women also fall victim to photoshopped images of other women in advertising campaigns. Advertising tells us what it means to be a desirable woman or man. Researchers have found that exposure to ultrathin models and celebrities on television and other media leads to increasing levels of body dissatisfaction and eating disorders in young women (e.g., Harrison & Cantor, 1997; Levine & Smolak, 1996; Thompson, Heinberg, Altabe, & Tantleff-Dunn, 1999). Because of the importance of thinness, women experience greater pressure to achieve this ideal. Psychologists have noted, "Opportunities for ... social comparison are ubiquitous, as everyday social interactions and the media inundate us with information about other people's accomplishments, actions, and lifestyles" (Lyubomirsky & Ross, 1997, p. 1141).

For example, Gonzales-Lavin and Smolak (1995) found that girls who spend more than 8 hours watching television per week reported significantly greater body-image dissatisfaction than girls with less television exposure. A survey study (Sheldon, 2010) with 122 female and 102 male college students revealed that although women read fashion magazines more often than men, the amount of time they spent reading them was not related to their body esteem. Rather, the comparison to models in those magazines was what made women have negative attitudes toward their bodies. In other words, women who *compare* themselves to models in magazines and are under high family and peer pressure to have perfect bodies end up having lower body esteem than women who are not under family or peer pressure. This was not the case with men. Cross and Madson (1997) argued that men tend to develop and maintain independent self-construal, and therefore they rely on other people's opinions less than women, thus protecting themselves from negative practices of social comparisons and trying to achieve the "ideal."

SOCIAL MEDIA

The widespread use of digital editing has expanded from public content such as advertisements and magazines to private use in personal social media accounts. One difference between social media images and images in magazines is the type of comparison targets that they contain. Thus while magazines generally feature images of models and celebrities, social media also features images of one's peers (Hew, 2011). Like magazine images, Facebook images can also be "enhanced" before publication. A variety of computer programs and apps allow for endless manipulation of images to the point that the image the audience sees does not resemble the actual photograph. Techniques such as airbrushing can remove any flaws on a face or body. Regular people can now make their waists look smaller and their breasts look bigger.

The increasing use of social media and social networking sites (SNSs) also changed which components of appearance were salient during the appearance comparison process (Fardouly, Diedrichs, Vartanian, & Halliwell, 2015). While traditional media focus primarily on the body, social media focus more on portrait pictures (Haferkamp, Eimler, Papadakis, & Kruck, 2012). This provides opportunities for women to make face-, skin-, and hair-related comparisons (Fardouly et al., 2015). In fact, in a study with female participants from a university in the United Kingdom, Fardouly et al. (2015) found that Facebook exposure was associated with face-, hair-, and skin-related concerns but not weight-related body dissatisfaction.

The use of social media has been linked to increased social comparison and diminished self-esteem. Self-esteem refers to a person's positive or negative evaluation of the self—that is, the extent to which an individual views the self as worthwhile and competent (Coopersmith, 1967). Vogel, Rose, Roberts, and Eckles (2014) did a study with undergraduate students to determine whether people who have greater exposure to upward social comparisons via SNSs have lower trait self-esteem. The results of their experimental study revealed that people who had the most chronic exposure to Facebook (i.e., used it most frequently) tended to have lower trait self-esteem. Moreover, the extent of upward social comparison on Facebook was greater than the extent of downward social comparison, and this extent of upward (but not downward) social comparison via Facebook significantly mediated the relationship between Facebook use and trait self-esteem.

Haferkamp et al. (2012) further explored self-presentation on SNSs in the context of gender. Their study found that women were more likely to use SNSs for comparing themselves with others and acquiring information, whereas men primarily used SNSs to look at other people's profiles to find friends. Thus a study by Chua and Chang (2016) with high school girls from Singapore revealed that all participants encountered upward and downward comparisons depending on the peer being observed. The girls agreed that peer comparison was "stupid," "unhealthy," and "unnecessary" and viewed it as "not making sense." Still, all the participants made remarks about how peer comparison can have unhealthy consequences and lead to unhealthy behaviors, including them going back and deleting social media photos with few likes due to "frustration or embarrassment" (Chua & Chang, 2016). Participants acknowledged that being visually perceived as the "best" on social media has become the norm and the only way to be "pretty enough" for peers. One's number of followers is another status setter. In the Chua and Chang (2016) study, pride came with an increase in followers, and disappointment followed a decrease in followers. A girl's status online and in her peer group was determined by likes and followers; lower numbers could cause the peer group to experience "anger, jealousy, inadequacy, and doubts about self-worth." 38% of the girls perceived intense competition and would try to ignore likes and follows so that they could avoid paying attention to their peers' beauty and popularity (Chua & Chang, 2016).

Haferkamp and Kramer (2011) investigated the effects of online profiles on SNSs in two studies. The first study found that participants had a more negative body image after being shown profile pictures of physically attractive individuals than those who had been shown profile pictures of less physically attractive individuals. The second study found that male participants who were shown profiles of more successful men reported a higher perceived divergence between their current career status and their ideal career status when compared with male participants who were shown profiles of less successful individuals.

Social media are visual and therefore most comparisons are in terms of physical appearance. Rutledge, Gillmor, and Gillen (2013) found that Facebook is more appealing to those who are concerned with their appearance, because it allows them to construct the image that they wish to portray to the public. Chou and Edge (2012), however, examined the impact of using social media on people's perceptions of others' lives. They found that those who used Facebook longer thought that others were happier and had better lives. This is due to availability heuristic. People make judgments about others based on other-generated descriptions, which can include comments left on someone's social media account (Walther, Van Der Heide, & Kim, 2008). This phenomenon might be common on social media where users may not know all of their friends closely.

Instagram. Instagram has a lot of features that might encourage social comparisons. First, unlike other social media outlets that are more text based (e.g., Twitter), Instagram focuses only on images. The two most common types of images shared on Instagram are selfies and photos of friends (Hu, Manikonda, & Kambhampati, 2014; Ridgway & Clayton, 2016). These types of posts can explicitly communicate beauty, but they also encourage social comparisons.

Studies have examined social comparison processes on Instagram. Hendrickse, Arpan, Clayton, and Ridgway (2017) found that individuals who engaged in more appearance-related comparisons on Instagram reported experiencing a more intense drive toward thinness and greater body dissatisfaction. Ahadzadeh, Pahlevan Sharif, and Ong (2017) also found that Instagram usage was negatively associated with body satisfaction for college students, especially those with lower levels of self-esteem. A survey of female undergraduate students revealed that acute exposure to *fitspiration* images on Instagram led to increased body dissatisfaction and decreased self-esteem (Tiggemann & Zaccardo, 2015).

A popular trend that has emerged on the Internet in recent years is "fitspiration." Fitspiration (a blending of the words "fitness" and "inspiration") arose as an antidote to the trend of "thinspiration" (a blending of "thinness" and "inspiration") (Ghaznavi & Taylor, 2015). Fitspiration consists of images and messages that purport to motivate people to exercise and pursue a healthier lifestyle (Abena, 2013), with a goal to encourage strength and female empowerment (Tiggemann & Zaccardo, 2015). However, studies have suggested that, just like thinspiration, fitspiration also promotes a homogenous body shape (tall, lean, toned, and "perfectly proportioned"), often contains guilt-inducing messages, and emphasizes dieting and restrictive eating (Boepple, Ata, Rum, & Thompson, 2016; Tiggemann & Zaccardo, 2016).

Most, if not all, previous studies have looked at appearance-related social comparisons. Sheldon and Wiegand (2018), however, did a study to explore how female college students use social media to compare themselves not only in terms of physical appearance but also school success, eating habits, exercise habits, happiness, intelligence, and popularity (see Table 4.2).

Sheldon and Wiegand (2018) found that women who compare themselves to other women on social media tend to have a lower body esteem (see Table 4.3).

TABLE 4.2 Comparison to Female Friends on Social Media Items

	M	SD
In general	3.15	1.03
In terms of school success	3.06	1.15
In terms of eating habits	2.68	1.27
In terms of exercise habits	2.99	1.20
In terms of happiness	3.06	1.12
In terms of intelligence	2.78	1.20
In terms of physical appearance	**3.46**	1.14
In terms of popularity	2.70	1.27
In terms of body weight	3.14	1.32
In terms of muscle tone	2.94	1.34

Note: Bold is the highest mean.
From Sheldon, P., & Wiegand, A. (2018). Comparing ourselves to friends on social media: The role of body esteem and Instagram gratifications. In: Paper presented at the Alabama Communication Association conference.

TABLE 4.3 Correlations Between Body Mass Index (BMI), Body Esteem, and Comparison to Friends on Social Media Items

Comparison to Friends on Social Media	BMI	Body Esteem
In general	0.09	−.44**
In terms of school success	0.11	−.20**
In terms of eating habits	0.04	−.31**
In terms of exercise habits	0.08	−.33**
In terms of happiness	−0.03	−.26**
In terms of intelligence	−0.11	−.26**
In terms of physical appearance	.16*	−.52**
In terms of popularity	−0.03	−.27**
In terms of body weight	.27**	−.52**
In terms of muscle tone	−0.01	−.23**

Note: p stands for significance: *p < .05; **p < .01.

Comparisons to female friends also influenced how women used Instagram. Thus comparison in terms of popularity was the only comparison category significantly related to the number of Instagram followers—indicating again that Instagram is all about self-promotion. Another study (Marcus, 2015) found that, unlike other SNSs, Instagram is based more on one's personal identity than their relational identity. Marcus (2015) analyzed the images that five individuals, ages 22–25, posted on Instagram and concluded that Instagram exists for people to self-promote—and, unlike Facebook, it does not focus on social relationships as much.

The study by Sheldon and Wiegand (2018) also found a positive relationship between socially interacting on Instagram and comparison in terms of popularity, physical appearance, body weight, and muscle tone. This reaffirms the common belief that Instagram is all about self-promotion and looks. Prior theories on the psychological development of emerging adults state that young adults tend to explore self-identity by seeking continuous approval from peers during the process (Arnett, 2004). This reflects the tenets of social comparison theory. In addition, those who make comparisons in terms of popularity, physical appearance, body weight, and muscle tone also engage in more frequent editing of their Instagram posts (Sheldon & Wiegand, 2018). This reveals how much effort one is putting into making sure they look as good as their friends and are as popular as them. It also reflects the tenets of social comparison theory.

PINTEREST

Pinterest is another popular image-sharing social network site. Pinterest allows users to upload, save, and manage images, also known as "pins" (visual bookmarks), through collections known as (pin)boards. Pinboards serve as big catalogs of objects. Users can create their own "boards" and "pin" images that they find while browsing the Internet. The boards can be organized into themes that reflect their individual style. Users can also tag or title the image and share it with their social network.

Pinterest users are predominantly young females and are therefore more likely to be exposed to images of other physically attractive and fit women. In fact, unlike other SNSs, Pinterest can be compared to a modern-day magazine. Most participants identify fashion as the main reason for Pinterest use. The topic of fashion includes items such as style, outfits, clothing, and shopping (Mittal, Gupta, Dewan, & Kumaraguru, 2013). Hair and Beauty is one of the top three categories for board creation, and Health and Fitness boards have the third most followers by pin (Mittal et al., 2013). These topics may heighten women's body image concerns.

Simpson and Mazzeo (2017) examined "fitspiration" (fitness and inspiration) messages on Pinterest and found that they encouraged weight management behavior and appearance-related body standards over health-related behavior and standards. These messages emphasized attractiveness as a motivation to partake in such behaviors. Fitspiration messages also included a comparable amount of fit praise (i.e., emphasis on toned/defined muscles) and thin praise (i.e., emphasis on slenderness). In another study (Lewallen & Behm-Morawitz, 2016), Pinterest users who followed more fitness boards were more likely to report intentions to engage in extreme weight loss behaviors.

Alperstein (2015) conducted a study with the goal of describing and explaining how women use idealized images of Western femininity displayed on Pinterest for social comparison. The study utilized the Pinterest site of Lauren Santo Domingo, who is one of the most widely followed individuals on Pinterest. Respondents were asked to look at the LSD "live" Pinterest page and review the pinboards that were linked to the main page. They were asked to react emotionally—in an open-ended manner—to the boards. They were asked to evaluate the pages comparing their own lives to that which is depicted on the pinboards. Four broad themes emerged from the research, indicating that respondents compared themselves to the images by viewing them as unattainable, viewing them with admiration, identifying similarities between the pinner and the respondents, and engaging in downward comparison—in which case the respondent looked at the pinboards with disdain. The upward comparison included both having admiration for the pinner and perhaps the desire to emulate her. However, the upward comparison also included the inability to reach the desired status. Alperstein (2015) described this as a double bind in which the desirable is pitted against the desired, which may lead to a depressive and perhaps somewhat hopeless state.

Selfie-editing. Image-based social media, such as Instagram and Snapchat, are popular outlets for selfie-posting. People use selfies to brag about their daily lives, while also carefully crafting their public persona. What is also rising is people's obsession with how to portray themselves on those sites. This is evident in the number of beautification apps that are available on the market (e.g., BeautyCam), but also in the prevalence of selfie-editing. Selfie-editing is defined as the digital enhancement of selfies using computer programs or smartphone applications (e.g., filters, teeth whitening, nose narrowing, slimming face, and removing dark circles around eyes) (Chae, 2017). It is an effort for the online presentation of the ideal self. A survey of 1710 American adults revealed that 50% of the respondents edit their selfies (Renfrew Center Foundation, 2014). Selfie-editing might negatively impact not only the presenters but also the audience. Those exposed to edited selfies might feel inadequate and pressured to change their appearances as well.

Selfie-editing is a means for selective self-presentation (Chae, 2017). It is the result of social comparison of appearance. Even celebrities edit their selfies before posting on Instagram. Selfies encourage people to take a closer look into their appearance. A survey among plastic surgeons revealed that patients are increasingly becoming aware of their facial appearance due to their selfies (American Academy of Facial Plastic and Reconstructive Surgery, 2014). Those who have a high awareness of the self are especially conscious. They worry about how they look and how others perceive their appearance and are therefore more likely to evaluate their appearance and engage in social comparison (Chae, 2017).

Chae (2017) conducted an online survey with Korean female smartphone users aged 20–39 in order to examine the psychological mechanism leading to selfie-editing. The results showed that selfie-taking frequency, public self-consciousness, and social media use at Wave 1 were associated with social comparison with friends at Wave 1—which increased selfie-editing behavior at Wave 2. Chae (2017) concluded that individuals edit their selfies not because they are dissatisfied with their appearance, but because they want to look better than others—or at least look like others based on social comparison. Greater use of social media implies more exposure to other people's selfies, which brings about social comparison. It appears that people who edit their selfies are comparison-oriented people with a high public self-consciousness who frequently take selfies and use social media (Chae, 2017).

Social Comparisons Among Teens. Teenagers are in the age-group that uses social media the most. They are also more susceptible to negative psychological and behavioral outcomes from social media use (Twyman, Saylor, Taylor, & Comeaux, 2010). They use social media for self-presentation and to impress others (Carpenter, 2012), which often causes psychological stress and narcissism, as well as social comparisons and envy (Chua & Chang, 2016). Smith and Kim (2007, p. 49) defined envy as "an unpleasant and often painful blend of feelings caused by a comparison with a group of persons who possess something we desire." Being exposed to information that our friends share on social media can trigger negative feelings about oneself, especially when that information is positive, as most social media posts are. Tandoc, Ferrucci, and Duffy (2015) found that college students who spent more time on Facebook tended to engage in what the authors labeled as *Facebook envy*. Individuals might perceive themselves as being inferior and think that other people lead more active and satisfying lives—which eventually results in envy (Chou & Edge, 2012; Krasnova, Wenninger, Widjaja, & Buxmann, 2013).

Social comparison and envy, however, are a result of the social environment that teenagers are in. Charoensukmongkol (2018) surveyed Thai teenagers between 13 and 19 years of age and found that teenagers who rated themselves higher on a social media use intensity measure tended to report a higher degree of social comparison and envy. Most importantly, the relationship between social media use intensity and these behavioral outcomes was strongly influenced by the social environment to which the teenagers belonged. Thus competition among friends in a peer group was a key factor influencing the tendency to engage in social comparison. Another factor that caused envy, but not social comparison, was parents' comparisons between children. Prior studies (e.g., Feinberg, Neiderhiser, Simmens, Reiss, & Hetherington, 2000) have found that parents comparing their own children with the children of others, or with the child's siblings, can lead to teenagers developing negative personalities and behaviors such as jealousy, sibling rivalry, and the loss of self-confidence. It also increases social comparison behavior.

CONCLUSION

The media's presentation of unrealistic physical proportions tends to hold devastating effects over everyone, but especially women in today's society (Cash & Henry, 1995). Researchers have started coming up with ideas to change this trend. One suggestion is to provide information about the unrealistic nature of media images. This includes teaching people visual literacy. Visual literacy is defined as "the ability to read, interpret, and understand information presented in pictorial or graphic images" (Wileman, 1993, p. 114). There is a lot of content on the Internet, which aims to teach people about how to spot obvious image editing, yet companies continue to improve and enhance their methods to make it impossible to notice retouching (Farid & Bravo, 2010). Instances of upward comparison may decrease once viewers understand that the subjects of the photos are not realistic. In fact, a study in which an intervention video was shown before exposure to media images completely got rid of the negative effects in adolescent girls (Halliwell, Easun, & Harcourt, 2011). Considering that there is growing evidence that young men may also be negatively affected by exposure to idealized media models (Barlett, Vowels, & Saucier, 2008; Blond, 2008), it is likely that similar interventions could benefit them.

In conclusion, we should all question social media messages and images we see. We need to ask ourselves the following questions: Who created them? Why? What techniques did they use? Using social media mindfully is actually the key to preventing the negative effects of social comparisons.

References

Abena. *From thinspo to fitspiration: How social media could be affecting your body image*. (2013). Retrieved from: <http://www.collegefashion.net/college-life/from-thinspo-to-fitspiration-how-social-media-could-be-affecting-your-body-image/>.

Ahadzadeh, A. S., Pahlevan Sharif, S., & Ong, F. S. (2017). Self-schema and self-discrepancy mediate the influence of Instagram usage on body image satisfaction among youth. *Computers in Human Behavior, 68*(Supplement C), 8−16. Available from https://doi.org/10.1016/j.chb.2016.11.011.

Alperstein, N. (2015). Social comparison of idealized female images and the curation of self on Pinterest. *The Journal of Social Media in Society, 4*(2), 5−27.

American Academy of Facial Plastic and Reconstructive Surgery. *Selfie trend increases demand for facial plastic surgery*. (2014). Retrieved from: <http://www.aafprs.org/media/press_release/20140311.html>.

Arnett, J. (2004). *Emerging adulthood: The winding roads from the late teens through the twenties.* New York, NY: Oxford University Press.

Bandura, A., & Jourden, F. J. (1991). Self-regulatory mechanisms governing the impact of comparison on complex decision making. *Journal of Personality, 60*, 941−951.

Barlett, C. P., Vowels, C. L., & Saucier, D. A. (2008). Meta-analyses of the effects of media images on men's body image concerns. *Journal of Social and Clinical Psychology, 27*, 279−310. Available from https://doi.org/10.1521/jscp.2008.27.3.279.

Blond, A. (2008). Impacts of exposure to images of ideal bodies on male body dissatisfaction: A review. *Body Image, 5*, 244−250. Available from https://doi.org/10.1016/j.bodyim.2008.02.003.

Boepple, L., Ata, R. N., Rum, R., & Thompson, J. K. (2016). Strong is the new skinny: A content analysis of fitspiration websites. *Body Image, 17*, 132−135. Available from https://doi.org/10.1016/j.bodyim.2016.03.001.

Buunk, B. E., VanYperen, N. W., Taylor, S. E., & Collins, R. L. (1991). Social comparison and the drive upward revisited: Affiliation as a response to marital stress. *European Journal of Social Psychology, 21*, 529−546.

Carpenter, C. J. (2012). Narcissism on Facebook: Self-promotional and anti-social behavior. *Personality and Individual Differences, 52*(4), 482−486.

Cash, T., & Henry, P. (1995). Women's body images: The result of a national survey in the USA. *Sex Roles: A Journal of Research, 33*, 19−26.

Chae, J. (2017). Virtual makeover: Selfie-taking and social media use increase selfie-editing frequency through social comparison. *Computers in Human Behavior, 66*, 370−376.

Charoensukmongkol, P. (2018). The impact of social media on social comparison and envy in teenagers: The moderating role of the parent comparing children and in-group competition among friends. *Journal of Child & Family Studies, 27*(1), 69–79. Available from https://doi.org/10.1007/s10826-017-0872-8.

Chou, H. G., & Edge, N. (2012). They are happier and having better lives than I am: The impact of using Facebook on perceptions of others' lives. *Cyberpsychology, Behavior & Social Networking, 15*(2), 117–121. Available from https://doi.org/10.1089/cyber.2011.0324.

Chua, T. H., & Chang, L. (2016). Follow me and like my beautiful selfies: Singapore teenage girls' engagement in self-presentation and peer comparison on social media. *Computer in Human Behavior, 55*, 190–197. Available from https://doi.org/10.1016/j.chb.2015.09.011.

Coopersmith, S. (1967). *The antecedents of self-esteem.* San Francisco, CA: Freeman.

Cross, S. E., & Madson, L. (1997). Models of the self: Self-construals and gender. *Psychological Bulletin, 122*, 5–37.

Fardouly, J., Diedrichs, P. C., Vartanian, L. R., & Halliwell, E. (2015). Social comparisons on social media: The impact of Facebook on young women's body image concerns and mood. *Body Image, 13*, 38–45.

Farid, H., & Bravo, M. J. (2010, January). Image forensic analyses that elude the human visual system. In: *Paper presented at the SPIE symposium on electronic imaging,* San Jose, CA.

Feinberg, M. E., Neiderhiser, J. M., Simmens, S., Reiss, D., & Hetherington, E. M. (2000). Sibling comparison of differential parental treatment in adolescence: Gender, self-esteem, and emotionality as mediators of the parenting-adjustment association. *Child Development, 71*(6), 1611–1628. Available from https://doi.org/10.1111/1467-8624.00252.

Festinger, L. (1954). A theory of social comparison processes. *Human Relations, 7*, 117–140. Available from https://doi.org/10.1177/001872675400700202.

Ghaznavi, J., & Taylor, L. D. (2015). Bones, body parts, and sex appeal: An analysis of #thinspiration images on popular social media. *Body Image, 14*, 54–61. Available from https://doi.org/10.1016/j.bodyim.2015.03.006.

Gonzales-Lavin, A., & Smolak, L. (1995). Relationship between television and eating problems in middle school girls. In: *Paper presented at the annual meeting of the Society for Research in Child Development,* Indianapolis, IN.

Haferkamp, N., Eimler, S. C., Papadakis, A., & Kruck, J. V. (2012). Men are from Mars, women are from Venus? Examining gender differences in self-presentation on social networking sites. *Cyberpsychology, Behavior, and Social Networking, 15*(2), 91–98.

Haferkamp, N., & Kramer, N. C. (2011). Social comparison 2.0: Examining the effects of online profiles on social-networking sites. *Cyberpsychology, Behavior, and Social Networking, 14*, 309–314.

Halliwell, E., Easun, A., & Harcourt, D. (2011). Body dissatisfaction: Can a short media literacy message reduce negative media exposure effects amongst adolescent girls? *British Journal of Health Psychology, 16*, 396–403. Available from https://doi.org/10.1348/135910710X515714.

Harrison, K., & Cantor, J. (1997). The relationship between media consumption and eating disorders. *Journal of Communication, 47*, 40–66.

Hendrickse, J., Arpan, L. M., Clayton, R. B., & Ridgway, J. L. (2017). Instagram and college women's body image: Investigating the roles of appearance-related comparisons and intrasexual competition. *Computers in Human Behavior, 74*, 92–100. Available from https://doi.org/10.1016/j.chb.2017.04.027.

Hew, K. F. (2011). Students' and teachers' use of Facebook. *Computers in Human Behavior*, 27, 662–676. Available from https://doi.org/10.1016/j.chb.2010.11.020.

Hu, Y., Manikonda, L., & Kambhampati, S. (2014). What we Instagram: A first analysis of Instagram photo content and user types. In: *Proceedings of the eighth international AAAI conference on weblogs and social media* (pp. 595–598). Association for the Advancement of Artificial Intelligence, Ann Arbor, MI.

Krasnova, H., Wenninger, H., Widjaja, T., & Buxmann, P. (2013). Envy on Facebook: A hidden threat to users' life satisfaction? In: *Paper presented at the 11th international conference on Wirtschaftsinformatik (WI)*, Leipzig, Germany.

Levine, M. P., & Smolak, L. (1996). Media as a context for the development of disordered eating. In L. Smolak, & M. P. Levine (Eds.), *The developmental psychopathology of eating disorders: Implications for research, prevention, and treatment* (pp. 235–257). Mahwah, NJ: Lawrence Erlbaum Associates, Inc.

Lewallen, J., & Behm-Morawitz, E. (2016). Pinterest or thinterest?: Social comparison and body image on social media. *Social Media in Society*, 2(1), 1–9. Available from https://doi.org/10.1177/2056305116640559.

Lockwood, P., Dolderrnan, D., Sadler, P., & Gerchak, E. (2004). Feeling better about doing worse: Social comparisons within romantic relationships. *Journal of Personality and Social Psychology*, 87, 80–95.

Lyubomirsky, S., & Ross, L. (1997). Hedonic consequences of social comparison: A contrast of happy and unhappy people. *Journal of Personality and Social Psychology*, 73, 1141–1157.

Marcus, S. R. (2015). Picturing' ourselves into being: Assessing identity, sociality and visuality on Instagram. In: *Presented at the International Communication Association conference*, San Juan, Puerto Rico.

Marsh, H. W., & Hau, K. (2003). Big-fish-little-pond effect on academic self-concept. A cross-cultural (26-country) test of the negative effects of academically selective schools. *American Psychologist*, 58, 364–376.

Marsh, H. W., & Parker, J. W. (1984). Determinants of student self-concept: Is it better to be a relatively large fish in a small pond even if you don't learn to swim as well? *Journal of Personality and Social Psychology*, 47, 213–231.

Mittal, S., Gupta, N., Dewan, P., & Kumaraguru, P. (2013). The pin-band theory: Discovering the Pinterest world. *Computing Research Repository*, arXiv preprint arXiv:1307.4952.

Renfrew Center Foundation. *Afraid to be your selfie?: Survey reveals most people photoshop their images.* (2014). Retrieved from: <http://renfrewcenter.com/news/afraid-be-your-selfie-survey-reveals-most-people-photoshop-their-images>.

Ridgway, J. L., & Clayton, R. B. (2016). Instagram unfiltered: Exploring associations of body image satisfaction, Instagram #Selfie posting, and negative romantic relationship outcomes. *Cyberpsychology, Behavior, and Social Networking*, 19(1), 2–7. Available from https://doi.org/10.1089/cyber.2015.0433.

Rutledge, C. M., Gillmor, K. L., & Gillen, M. M. (2013). Does this profile picture make me look fat? Facebook and body image in college students. *Psychology of Popular Media Culture*, 2, 251–258. Available from https://doi.org/10.1037/ppm0000011.

Sheldon, P. (2010). Pressure to be perfect: Influences on college students' body esteem. *Southern Communication Journal*, 75, 277–298. Available from https://doi.org/10.1080/10417940903026543.

Sheldon, P., & Wiegand, A. (2018). Comparing ourselves to friends on social media: The role of body esteem and Instagram gratifications. In: *Paper presented at the Alabama Communication Association conference*.

Simpson, C. C., & Mazzeo, S. E. (2017). Skinny is not enough: A content analysis of fitspiration on Pinterest. *Health Communication, 32*(5), 560–567. Available from https://doi.org/10.1080/10410236.2016.1140273.

Smith, R. H., & Kim, S. H. (2007). Comprehending envy. *Psychological Bulletin, 133*, 46–64.

Tandoc, E. C., Jr, Ferrucci, P., & Duffy, M. (2015). Facebook use, envy, and depression among college students: Is facebooking depressing? *Computers in Human Behavior, 43*, 139–146. Available from https://doi.org/10.1016/j.chb.2014.10.053.

Taylor, S. E., & Lobel, M. (1989). Social comparison activity under threat: Downward evaluation and upward contacts. *Psychological Review, 96*, 569–575.

Thompson, J. K., Heinberg, L. J., Altabe, M., & Tantleff-Dunn, S. (1999). *Exacting beauty: Theory, assessment, and treatment of body image disturbance.* Washington, DC: APA.

Tiggemann, M., & Zaccardo, M. (2015). Exercise to be fit, not skinny: The effect of fitspiration imagery on women's body image. *Body Image, 15*, 61–67. Available from https://doi.org/10.1016/j.bodyim.2015.06.003.

Tiggemann, M., & Zaccardo, M. (2016). 'Strong is the new skinny': A content analysis of #fitspiration images on Instagram. *Journal of Health Psychology*, 1–9. Available from https://doi.org/10.1177/1359105316639436.

Twyman, K., Saylor, C., Taylor, L. A., & Comeaux, C. (2010). Comparing children and adolescents engaged in cyberbullying to matched peers. *Cyberpsychology, Behavior, and Social Networking, 13*(2), 195–199.

Vogel, E. A., Rose, J. P., Roberts, L. R., & Eckles, K. (2014). Social comparison, social media, and self-esteem. *Psychology of Popular Media Culture, 3*, 206–222.

Walther, J. B., Van Der Heide, B., Kim, S., et al. (2008). The role of friends' appearance and behavior: Are we known by the company we keep? *Human Communication Research, 3*, 28–49.

Wert, S. R., & Salovey, P. (2004). A social comparison account of gossip. *Review of General Psychology, 8*, 122–137.

Wileman, R. E. (1993). *Visual communicating.* Englewood Cliffs, NJ: Educational Technology Publications.

Social Media and Relationship Drama

ROMANTIC RELATIONSHIP PROBLEMS

Jealousy

Jealousy is a "complex of thoughts, feelings, and actions which follow threats to self-esteem and/or threats to the existence or quality of the relationship" (White, 1981, p. 129). According to Pfeiffer and Wong (1989), jealousy construct consists of three dimensions: emotional, cognitive, and behavioral. Affective/emotional jealousy involves the experience of negative emotions directed at relationship threats. Cognitive jealousy involves the appraisal of relational threats or suspicions regarding a romantic partner's infidelity. Behavioral jealousy consists of protective actions that individuals engage in to "check up on" romantic partners. Romantic jealousy is a complex emotion comprised different parts, including anger, sadness, and fear caused by a partner's suspected or actual infidelity (Hudson et al., 2015).

According to Bevan (2013), social media are a fertile ground for romantic jealousy as they provide a centralized place to survey romantic partners' social connection and behavior and make it easier to maintain relationships with romantic rivals. Social network sites also collapse contexts, generating more ambiguous social situations that could result in misinterpretations. Elphinston and Noller (2011) found that people with an excessive and dysfunctional attachment to Facebook tended to exhibit more jealous thoughts and engaged more frequently in surveillance of romantic partners. The more time someone spends on Facebook, the more Facebook jealousy they experience (Muise, Christofides, & Desmarais, 2009). In addition, studies show that women experience more Facebook jealousy than men, as well as a more profound emotional response. Men generally exhibit a more violent or aggressive behavioral response (Buss & Schmitt, 1993). Women also react more strongly to cues indicating emotional infidelity, whereas men react more strongly to cues indicating sexual infidelity. Men are also more jealous of cybersex than emotional cheating, whereas women displayed the opposite trend (Buss & Schmitt, 1993). However, the higher relationship trust, the lower Facebook jealousy is (Muise et al., 2009).

Nongpong and Charoensukmongkol (2016) surveyed both married and single individuals to determine the consequences of excessive use of social media. Those included (1) loneliness, (2) lack of caring, and (3) jealousy. The authors found that those who perceived that their partners used social media excessively tended to report a lack of caring, loneliness, and jealousy. In addition, the perception of relationship problems associated with social media use by own partners was more severe for the respondents who reported that they used social media less intensively than their partners. Conversely, for the respondents who reported that they used social media to a greater degree than their partners, the impacts on the perceived relationship problems were significantly lessened.

The lack of nonverbal cues in computer-mediated communication has led to the use of emoticons. They are used to convey emotional meanings in text-based applications. Emoticons also have the potential to significantly alter the interpretation of a message. Hudson et al. (2015) examined whether gender and emoticons interacted to influence Facebook jealousy. They conducted three studies, and in each of the studies, the participants were asked to respond to a scripted scenario of being in a committed relationship, borrowing their significant other's laptop, and finding a message from the opposite sex in the Facebook inbox stating, "What are you up to later?" The control condition featured the absence of an emoticon, while the experimental condition featured an emoticon to accompany the message. The first study results revealed that men displayed higher jealousy scores than women with a winking emoticon while women scored higher with the absence of an emoticon. Study 2 included 111 (51 males and 60 females) college students, and the participants completed the Facebook Jealousy Scale. The results revealed females scoring higher in jealousy than males.

A study with Dutch college students (Utz & Beukeboom, 2011) revealed that low self-esteem individuals experienced more social media jealousy than high self-esteem individuals. Most participants admitted that they would monitor a partner's social networking site (SNS) profile but less likely never engage in traditional monitoring behavior such as searching the partner's bags or secretly reading the partner's e-mails.

Cohen, Bowman, and Borchert (2014) examined how SNS message exclusivity affects jealousy. The participants reacted to a hypothetical situation of discovering their romantic partner communicating with an ex on Facebook. The sample size consisted of 191 undergraduate students from a mid-Atlantic university. The findings indicated that participants felt more threatened with private messages as it signifies communication behind "closed doors." Private message viewers were also more likely to confront their partner. Both negative emotions and threat perceptions gave rise to confrontations.

Dialectic Tensions

Relational dialectics theory (RDT) has been used in understanding the potential influence of Facebook on romantic relationships. The RDT (Baxter & Montgomery, 1996) is an interpersonal communication theory that explains communication patterns that arise between individuals when they maintain a relationship. According to the theory, partners must try to balance the effects of forces acting to simultaneously bring them together and pull them apart. These forces manifest as discursive struggles known as *dialectics*. Dialectics occur both internally (within the couple) and externally (between the couple and their social networks; Baxter, 1990). Three primary dialectics include integration—separation (i.e., autonomy—connection), stability—change (i.e., predictability—novelty), and expression—privacy (i.e., openness—closeness).

The most salient of the three primary dialectics is expression—privacy. Some individuals are willing to post large quantities of information about their relationship online, whereas other partners might be less comfortable doing so. Couples must work together to balance the expression of privacy within the relationship and between the couple and their broader social network (Fox, Osborn, & Warber, 2014). Fox, Osborn, and Warber (2014) conducted 10 focus groups with 47 (23 men and 24 women) Midwestern university students. The participants were asked questions such as "What kind of benefits does Facebook have for romantic relationships?" The participants were also asked to draw from personal and nonpersonal experiences while answering. The participants collectively described Facebook as having a negative effect on romantic relationships overall. First, going or not going Facebook official (FBO) had often caused problems in relationships offline. One partner's unwillingness to publicly display their relationship status would almost always be negatively perceived by both the other partner as well as the online public. On the contrary, some participants reported that some couple employ the opposite of going FBO by not displaying relationship information at all—including pictures, statuses, or even friending their significant other. Going FBO was also seen as important to keep other competitors from pursuing their partners. Thus going FBO reflects a struggle between integration and separation within the couple that is also toed to the external privacy—expression dialectic.

Facebook is often credited with exacerbating relationship distress as evidenced by the ability to express that distress with the "It's Complicated" status. Some partners reported that they know others who use Facebook to intentionally manipulate and worry people, such as by posting older pictures with their ex-partners (Fox et al., 2014).

Infidelity

Increased Facebook and Twitter use is positively correlated with marital problems and rising divorce rates (Abbasi & Alghamdi, 2017; Clayton, 2014; Valenzuela, Halpern, & Katz, 2014). In many cases, divorce documents have listed Facebook infidelity as the grounds for divorce (Lumpkin, 2012). Individuals in unhappy marriages may use social network sites such as Facebook more often, because it provides them with social support (Mikal, Rice, Abeyta, & DeVilbiss, 2013). The most common reason for divorce via Facebook is flirtation. Virtual flirtations elicit physical and sexual reactions that are stronger than in a regular face-to-face interaction (Alapack, Blichfeldt, & Elden, 2005). Another reason for Facebook divorce is through infidelity. Infidelity is defined as "interactions in a relationship in which at least one of the people engaging in it understands there to be a violation of agreed or implicit sexual and/or emotional boundaries within their couple relationship" (Daines, 2006, p. 48). The most common source of Internet infidelity is an emotional affair (Hertlein & Piercy, 2006). Studies have shown that factors, such as an emotional and/or sexual disconnection and dissatisfaction in the primary relationship, are contributing to Internet infidelity (Mileham, 2007; Young, 2006).

Millner (2008) has theorized that a climate of relationship difficulties or "emotional sterility" in a couple relationship contributes to seeking "intimacy with detachment," or connecting with Internet partners. Two recent online surveys with Twitter (Clayton, 2014) and Facebook users (Clayton, Nagurney, & Smith, 2013) indicate that frequent relationship conflicts caused by the high levels of Facebook or Twitter usage by one partner can be associated with an increased risk of emotional or physical cheating and relationship breakup. Studies have looked at the effect of Internet infidelity on couple and family relationships. The findings show that Internet-based sex can lead to a loss of trust in the partner and a need to seek professional help to cope with the negative impact (Schneider, Weiss, & Samenow, 2012).

Cavaglion and Rashty (2010) analyzed 1130 messages from female members of two web-based Italian self-help groups for male cybersex and cyberporn dependents and their female partners. The participants' narratives showed a major pattern of distress, mainly related to ambivalent emotions and experiences of loss.

Finally, Cravens, Leckie, and Whiting (2013) used a grounded theory approach to analyze 90 stories about cheating written by receiving partners and posted on the "FacebookCheating" website. The stories revealed strong emotional reactions to the discovery of inadequate Facebook activities, with a common expression of emotional pain and feelings of hurt, loss of trust, shock and anger, and a struggle with the decision to end the relationship or not. Among the warning sings, nonparticipating partners often commented on an underlying "gut" feeling that something was amiss with their partner or in their relationship. They also noticed changes in their partner's behavior before or during the time when the infidelity behavior occurred. Suspicious and secretive behavior was also noted and included things such as closing out computer windows when one's partner came into a room, befriending past partners on Facebook, and concealing messages or text conversations. Many of the participants in the Cravens et al. (2013) study discussed discovering their partners' behaviors because their computers were left open with their Facebook accounts logged into.

Cyber cheating is a new phenomenon that has resulted from it being easier for users of the Internet to engage others romantically or flirtatiously in a discreet forum. A study (Helsper & Whitty, 2010) with 920 married couples reported that falling in love, engaging in cybersex, flirting, and revealing personal details to other parties were the most agreed-upon online infidelity behaviors. Cravens et al. (2013) found the following Facebook-related infidelity behaviors: friending one's ex-partner, private messaging, commenting on attractive users' pictures, and posting an inaccurate relationship status.

Abuse and Violence

Abusive and controlling behavior in romantic relationships can be facilitated through electronic communication technology, including social media. The most common technology-assisted dating violence and abuse include checking the partner's messages without permission, checking the whereabouts of the partner, demanding passwords for online accounts, deleting or unfriending ex-partners, using information posted online against the partner, pressuring partners to engage in sexual acts, insults or put downs, spreading rumors about the partner on the Internet, threatening the partner via ECT, sharing private or embarrassing images or videos of the partner, making the partner feel afraid not to respond to contact, and restricting the partner's electronic communication technology (ECT) use (Stonard, Walker, Bowen, & Price, 2017).

Attaching theory (Bowlby, 1977) has been used to explain abusive behavior within intimate relationships. Research with adults found that combinations of anxiously attached females (those who have a greater need for physical or emotional proximity) and avoidance-attached males (those who maintain greater distance) were associated with more violence (Doumas, Pearson, Elgin, & McKinley, 2008; Godbout, Dutton, Lussier, & Sabourin, 2009).

Relationship Dissolution

Relationship dissolution is a normal part of the relationship life cycle. According to Duck's (1982) relational dissolution model, partners experience the demise of a relationship through five phases: intrapsychic, dyadic, social, grave dressing, and resurrection. The *intrapsychic* process focuses on the partner as an internal desire by one or both partners, which stems from an individualistic reflection about the state of the relationship. The *dyadic* process focuses on the relationship and transpires when the two partners discuss their problems. At this stage they can choose to dissolve, repair, or postpone the relationship. After termination, news of the breakup is communicated to outside parties in the *social* process. *Grave dressing* is the next step and focuses on tidying up the accounts representing explanations for past actions and events. Tong (2013) posited that Facebook breakup disclosures likely happen during the grave dressing phase. Lastly, the new version of the model (Rollie & Duck, 2006) discusses the *resurrection* process, which focuses on the potential lessons learned from the previous relationship. LeFebvre, Blackburn, and Brody (2015) applied the relationship dissolution model by examining how collegiate Facebook users enact behaviors in breakups to extend the model to online environments during and after breakups. Their sample consisted of 208 undergraduate students.

On average the relationships reported ended 10.92 months prior to the study. The average time as a Facebook user was 47.6 months, and the average time per day spent on Facebook was 116.09 minutes.

The results produced two categories of responses—during dissolution and after dissolution. The top three behaviors in the during dissolution category are as follows: (1) 22.7% relational cleansing (hid, delay, removed relationship status; updated status to "Single" or "It's Complicated"; untagged or deleted wall postings and pictures/albums), (2) 22.6% minimal or no Facebook (no Facebook activity or limited Facebook activity), and (3) 10.2% surveillance (stalked and crept through their partner's social network and mutual friends' profiles). The same top three applied in the after dissolution category with respective percentages, (1) 20.4% relational cleansing, (2) 19.9% minimal or no Facebook impact (not affected by the breakup), and (3) 10.2% surveillance. The results also showed that participants appeared to reflect their psychological state in one of the four ways: (1) virtually mourning, (2) acknowledging with relational cleansing behaviors, (3) rumination through surveillance, and (4) distancing themselves through self-regulation. In addition, those who reported no Facebook-related behaviors in response to breakups indicated a higher level of postbreakup adjustment than those who utilized Facebook during and after breakups (LeFebvre et al., 2015).

Postbreakup

Breakups are challenging for many people, as one's identity changes from that of a couple to a single person. The nature of social media allows users to "creep" on ex-lovers following the breakup, which can prolong the mourning process (Fox et al., 2014). As relationships dissolve, the participants report that partners have to find ways to differentiate or separate from their ex-lover (Fox et al., 2014). Facebook was reported as being used to promote these situations by allowing the changing of relationship statuses. The participants also reported that the online evidence of the relationship (statuses, photos, mutual friend networks, etc.) made moving on especially difficult.

Haimson, Andalibi, Choudhury, and Hayes (2018) surveyed 119 US Facebook users who reported experiencing a recent breakup. They found that most participants (53%) considered the change of their relationship status as a primary Facebook disclosure method. About 46% indicated sending a private message to friend(s). Only 12% would publicly announce a breakup. In regards to the management of photos and statuses including a previous romantic partner, the majority (72%) indicated that they would leave them as is. In addition, most participants admitted that they were reluctant to share negative emotions due to self-presentation concerns.

Maintaining connections with an ex-partner through social media, however, increases negative effects and delays recovery and personal growth (Marshall, 2012). Yet, recent estimates suggest that one-half to two-thirds of people have made contact with an ex-partner through Facebook (Chaulk & Jones, 2011; Lyndon, Bonds-Raacke, & Cratty, 2011). Many of them find it to be harmless (Bowe, 2010). The reason they stay connected is attachment anxiety. Attachment theory (Bowlby, 1969) posits that the relationships one experiences with primary caregivers early in life shape how our adult relationships unfold across our lifespans. Two dimensions of attachment—anxiety and avoidance—can explain how one approaches close relationships (Bowlby, 1969). Thus studies have found that attachment avoidance is associated with minimizing contact with the partner (Davis, Shaver, & Vernon, 2003), whereas attachment anxiety is associated with greater preoccupation with the ex-partner. Attachment anxiety is also positively associated with Facebook surveillance, whereas attachment avoidance is negatively related to it (Marshall, Bejanyan, Di Castro, & Lee, 2013).

Marshall (2012) examined whether continued online contact with an ex-partner through Facebook inhibits adjustment and growth after a breakup. The study also examined the negative role of surveillance on Facebook in romantic relationships. The sample consisted of 464 (16% male and 84% female) participants, and results revealed that Facebook surveillance was associated with current distress over breakups, negative feelings, sexual desire, longing for the ex, and lower personal growth. Facebook provides information about ex-partners, which serves as a means for intensifying heartbreak. For example, seeing an ex establish a new relationship might have a negative effect on the partner surveilling. On the contrary, results showed that those who remained friends on Facebook with their exes were lower in negative feelings, sexual desire, and longing for their former partner than those who weren't Facebook friends. Overall, Marshall's (2012) results suggest that exposure to an ex-partner through Facebook may negatively affect healing and adjustments after the breakup.

PROBLEMS IN FRIENDSHIP RELATIONSHIPS

Unfriending

A Facebook profile owner with more friends is perceived more attractive than those with fewer Facebook friends. Tong, Van Der Heide, Langwell, and Walther (2008) found that the optimum number of friends in relation to social attractiveness was approximately 302. Being unfriended on Facebook can therefore be seen as negatively related to one's social and physical attractiveness (Bevan, Pfyl, & Barclay, 2012). The Oxford American Dictionary named "unfriend" their 2009 word of the year (Oxford word of the year: Unfriend, 2009). However, unfriending is a common Facebook behavior (Madden, 2012). It is a form of relationship termination. The termination can arouse rumination, or mulling, which is defined as "conscious thinking directed toward a given object for an extended period of time" (Gold & Wegner, 1995, p. 1246).

Bevan et al. (2012) did a survey study with adult individuals to learn about negative emotional and cognitive responses to being unfriended on Facebook. The sample size consisted of 547 adults aged 18 or older through an online questionnaire. The average age was 26.72 years. Bevan et al. (2012) found that the more preoccupied individuals were about their relationship, the more rumination and negative emotions they experienced posttermination. Being unfriended by someone close, such as family members and current or former friends or romantic partners, was associated with a greater rumination than being unfriended by more distant Facebook friends. In addition, when individuals could identify who their unfriender was, they experienced more rumination and negative emotions. In addition, ruminative and negative emotional responses were greatest when individuals perceived that they were unfriended for Facebook-related reasons—although the most frequent reason for unfriending was an upsetting offline event.

Expectancy violations theory (Burgoon & Jones, 1976) was used in previous studies (e.g., Bevan, Ang, & Fearns, 2014) to explain Facebook unfriending. According to the theory, human interaction is driven by expectations. Expectations for human behavior are learned. People learn their expectations from the culture in which they were born. When expectations are violated, the violation is judged as either positive or negative, depending on the reward potential of others. Bevan et al. (2014) found that Facebook unfriending is a computer-mediated behavior that individuals who have been unfriended perceive to be an expectancy violation that is moderately negative and moderately to highly important. Unfriended individuals are more likely to view these expectancy violations as more negative in valence when the unfriender was someone with whom they shared close ties (Bevan et al., 2014). The study also found that those who did contact the individual about being unfriended reported being moderately to highly satisfied with this interaction. In addition, females were more likely to view Facebook unfriending negatively than males were, and younger individuals perceived this act as a more expected expectancy violation than older individuals (Bevan et al., 2014).

Research shows that politics is the second most common reason for unfriending on social network sites (Rainie & Smith, 2012; Sibona, 2014). Individuals who are more politically engaged are also more likely to unfriend or unfollow someone. Individuals in more collectivistic cultures are less likely to engage in unfollowing or unfriending due to their goals to achieve group harmony (Skoric, Zhu, & Lin, 2018).

Political disagreements on social media are likely to trigger a defense motivation (Skoric et al., 2018). This can be explained by cognitive dissonance theory (Festinger, 1957). People try to justify their own opinions and therefore engage in selectivity bias, including selective avoidance of those who disagree with them. Thus exposure to dissonant political information on social media increases the chance of unfriending and unfollowing, especially if we disagree with strangers or people we consider to be "weak" ties (Skoric et al., 2018).

CONCLUSION

Social media have changed the way intimate relationships are initiated, maintained, and dissolved. This chapter provided an overview of the problems that technology use causes in both romantic and friendship relationships, including jealousy, infidelity, monitoring, controlling, and unfriending. While there is plenty of anecdotal evidence about how social media negatively influence interpersonal relationships, very few studies have explored those effects. Most research focuses on jealousy and stalking (Chapter 3: Cyberstalking and Bullying, discusses cyberstalking and cyberbullying).

References

Abbasi, I. S., & Alghamdi, N. G. (2017). When flirting turns into infidelity: The Facebook dilemma. *American Journal of Family Therapy, 45*(1), 1−14. Available from https://doi.org/10.1080/01926187.2016.1277804.

Alapack, R., Blichfeldt, M. F., & Elden, A. (2005). Flirting on the internet and the hickey: A hermeneutic. *Cyberpsychology & Behavior, 8*(1), 52−61.

Baxter, L. A. (1990). Dialectical contradictions in relationship development. *Journal of Social & Personal Relationships, 7,* 69−88. Available from https://doi.org/10.1177/0265407590071004.

Baxter, L. A., & Montgomery, B. M. (1996). *Relating: Dialogues and dialectics.* New York: Guilford.

Bevan, J. L. (2013). *The communication of jealousy.* New York: Peter Lang Publishing.

Bevan, J. L., Ang, P., & Fearns, J. B. (2014). Being unfriended on Facebook: An application of expectancy violation theory. *Computers in Human Behavior, 33,* 171−178. Available from https://doi.org/10.1016/j.chb.2014.01.029.

Bevan, J. L., Pfyl, J., & Barclay, B. (2012). Negative emotional and cognitive responses to being unfriended on Facebook: An exploratory study. *Computers in Human Behavior, 28*(4), 1458−1464. Available from https://doi.org/10.1016/j.chb.2012.03.008.

Bowe, G. (2010). Reading romance: The impact Facebook rituals can have on a romantic relationship. *Journal of Comparative Research in Anthropology and Sociology, 1,* 61−77.

Bowlby, J. (1969). Attachment and loss, vol. 1: Attachment. New York: Basic Books.

Bowlby, J. (1977). The making and breaking of affectional bonds. I. Aetiology and psychopathology in the light of attachment theory. An expanded version of the Fiftieth Maudsley Lecture, delivered before the Royal College of Psychiatrists, 19 November 1976. *British Journal of Psychiatry, 130,* 201−210. Available from https://doi.org/10.1192/bjp.130.3.201.

Burgoon, J. K., & Jones, S. B. (1976). Toward a theory of personal space expectations and their violations. *Human Communication Research, 2*, 131–146.

Buss, D. M., & Schmitt, D. P. (1993). Sexual strategies theory: An evolutionary perspective on human mating. *Psychological Review, 100*, 204–232.

Cavaglion, G., & Rashty, E. (2010). Narratives of suffering among Italian female partners of cybersex and cyber-porn dependents. *Sexual Addiction & Compulsivity: The Journal of Treatment & Prevention, 17*, 270–287.

Chaulk, K., & Jones, T. (2011). Online obsessive relational intrusion: Further concerns about Facebook. *Journal of Family Violence, 26*, 245–254.

Clayton, R. B. (2014). The third wheel: The impact of Twitter use on relationship infidelity and divorce. *Cyberpsychology, Behavior, and Social Networking, 17*(7), 425–430.

Clayton, R. B., Nagurney, A., & Smith, J. R. (2013). Cheating, breakup, and divorce: Is Facebook use to blame? *Cyberpsychology, Behavior and Social Networking, 16*, 717–720. Available from https://doi.org/10.1089/cyber.2012.0424.

Cohen, E. L., Bowman, N. D., & Borchert, K. (2014). Private flirts, public friends: Understanding romantic jealousy responses to an ambiguous social network site message as a function of message access exclusivity. *Computers in Human Behavior, 35*, 535–541. Available from https://doi.org/10.1016/j.chb.2014.02.050.

Cravens, J. D., Leckie, K. R., & Whiting, J. B. (2013). Facebook infidelity: When poking becomes problematic. *Contemporary Family Therapy, 35*(1), 74–90. Available from https://doi.org/10.1007/s10591-012-9231-5.

Daines, B. (2006). Violations of agreed and implicit sexual and emotional boundaries in couple relationships—Some thoughts arising from Levine's "A clinical perspective on couple infidelity.". *Sexual and Relationship Therapy, 21*, 45–53. Available from https://doi.org/10.1080/14681990500430011.

Davis, D., Shaver, P. R., & Vernon, M. L. (2003). Physical, emotional, and behavioral reactions to breaking up: The roles of gender, age, emotional involvement, and attachment style. *Personality & Social Psychology Bulletin, 29*, 871–884.

Doumas, D. M., Pearson, C. L., Elgin, J. E., & McKinley, L. L. (2008). Adult attachment as a risk factor for intimate partner violence: The "mispairing" of partners' attachment styles. *Journal of Interpersonal Violence, 23*, 616–634. Available from https://doi.org/10.1177/0886260507313526.

Duck, S. W. (1982). A topography of relationship disengagement and dissolution. In S. W. Duck (Ed.), *Personal relationship: Vol. 4. Dissolving personal relationships* (pp. 1–30). London, UK: Academic Press.

Elphinston, R. A., & Noller, P. (2011). Time to face it! Facebook intrusion and the implications for romantic jealousy and relationship satisfaction. *CyberPsychology, Behavior, and Social Networking, 14*, 631–635. Available from https://doi.org/10.1089/cyber.2010.0318.

Festinger, L. (1957). *A theory of cognitive dissonance*. CA: Stanford University Press.

Fox, J., Osborn, J. L., & Warber, K. M. (2014). Relational dialectics and social networking sites: The role of Facebook in romantic relationship escalation, maintenance, conflict, and dissolution. *Computers in Human Behavior, 35*, 527–534. Available from https://doi.org/10.1016/j.chb.2014.02.031.

Godbout, N., Dutton, D. G., Lussier, Y. A., & Sabourin, S. (2009). Early exposure to violence, domestic violence, attachment representations, and marital adjustment. *Personal Relationships, 16*, 365–384. Available from https://doi.org/10.1111/j.1475-6811.2009.01228.x.

Gold, D. B., & Wegner, D. M. (1995). Origins of ruminative thought: Trauma, incompleteness, nondisclosure, and suppression. *Journal of Applied Social Psychology, 25*, 1245–1261.

Haimson, O. L., Andalibi, N., Choudhury, M. D., & Hayes, G. R. (2018). Relationship breakup disclosures and media ideologies on Facebook. *New Media & Society, 20*(5), 1931–1952. Available from https://doi.org/10.1177/1461444817711402.

Helsper, E. J., & Whitty, M. T. (2010). Netiquette within married couples: Agreement about acceptable online behavior and surveillance between partners. *Computers in Human Behavior, 26*(5), 916–926. Available from https://doi.org/10.1016/j.chb.2010.02.006.

Hertlein, K. M., & Piercy, F. P. (2006). Internet infidelity: A critical review of the literature. *Family Journal, 14*(4), 366–371. Available from https://doi.org/10.1177/10664 80706290508.

Hudson, M. B., Nicolas, S. C., Howser, M. E., Lipsett, K. E., Robinson, I. W., Pope, L. J., ... Friedman, D. R. (2015). Examining how gender and emoticons influence Facebook jealousy. *Cyberpsychology, Behavior, and Social Networking, 18*(2), 87–92. Available from https://doi.org/10.1089/cyber.2014.0129.

LeFebvre, L., Blackburn, K., & Brody, N. (2015). Navigating romantic relationships on Facebook: Extending the relationship dissolution model to social networking environments. *Journal of Social and Personal Relationships, 32*(1), 78–98. Available from https://doi.org/10.1177/0265407514524848.

Lumpkin, S. (2012). Can Facebook ruin your marriage? *ABC World News.* Retrieved from: <http://abcnews.go.com/Technology/facebookrelationshipstatus/story?iD16406245#.T8e029PE>.

Lyndon, A., Bonds-Raacke, J., & Cratty, A. D. (2011). College students' Facebook stalking of ex-partners. *Cyberpsychology, Behavior, and Social Networking, 14*, 711–716.

Madden, M. (2012). *Privacy management on social media sites.* Pew Research Center's Internet and American Life Project. Retrieved from: <http://www.pewinternet.org/~/media//Files/Reports/2012/PIP_Privacy_management_on_social_media_sites_022412.pdf>.

Marshall, T. C. (2012). Facebook surveillance of former romantic partners: associations with postbreakup recovery and personal growth. *Cyberpsychology, Behavior, & Social Networking, 15*, 521–526.

Marshall, T. C., Bejanyan, K., Di Castro, G., & Lee, R. A. (2013). Attachment styles as predictors of Facebook-related jealousy and surveillance in romantic relationships. *Personal Relationships* (20, pp. 1–22).

Mikal, J. P., Rice, R. E., Abeyta, A., & DeVilbiss, J. (2013). Transition, stress and computer-mediated social support. *Computers in Human Behavior, 29*(5), A40–A53. Available from https://doi.org/10.1016/j.chb.2012.12.012.

Mileham, B. L. A. (2007). Online infidelity in Internet chat rooms: An ethnographic exploration. *Computers in Human Behavior, 23*, 11–31.

Millner, V. S. (2008). Internet infidelity: A case of intimacy with detachment. *The Family Journal, 16*, 78–82.

Muise, A., Christofides, E., & Desmarais, S. (2009). More information than you ever wanted: Does Facebook bring out the green-eyed monster of jealousy? *CyberPsychology & Behavior, 12*, 441–444. Available from https://doi.org/10.1089/cpb.2008.0263.

Nongpong, S., & Charoensukmongkol, P. (2016). I don't care much as long as I am also on Facebook: Impacts of social media use of both partners on romantic relationship problems. *The Family Journal, 24*(4), 351–358. Available from https://doi.org/10.1177/1066480716663199.

Oxford Word of the Year 2009: Unfriend. (2009). Retrieved from: <http://blog.oup.com/2009/11/unfriend/>.

Pfeiffer, S. M., & Wong, P. T. P. (1989). Multidimensional jealousy. *Journal of Social and Personal Relationships, 6*, 181–196. Available from https://doi.org/10.1177/02654 0758900600203.

Rainie, L., & Smith, A. (2012). *Social networking sites and politics.* Retrieved from: <http://www.pewinternet.org/2012/03/12/social-networking-sites-and-politics/>.

Rollie, S. S., & Duck, S. W. (2006). Divorce and dissolution of romantic relationships: Stage models and their limitations. In M. A. Fine, & J. H. Harvey (Eds.), *Handbook of divorce and relationship dissolution* (pp. 223–240). Mahwah, NJ: Lawrence Erlbaum Associates, Inc.

Schneider, J. P., Weiss, R., & Samenow, C. (2012). Is it really cheating? Understanding the emotional reactions and clinical treatment of spouses and partners affected by cybersex infidelity. *Sexual Addiction & Compulsivity: The Journal of Treatment & Prevention, 19,* 123–139.

Sibona, C. *Unfriending on Facebook: Context collapse and unfriending behaviors.* (2014). Retrieved from: <http://ieeexplore.ieee.org/stamp/stamp.jsp?tp = &arnumber = 6758811>.

Skoric, M. M., Zhu, Q., & Lin, J. T. (2018). What predicts selective avoidance on social media? A study of political unfriending in Hong Kong and Taiwan. *American Behavioral Scientist, 62*(8), 1097–1115. Available from https://doi.org/10.1177/0002764218764251.

Stonard, K. E., Bowen, E., Walker, K., & Price, S. A. (2017). "They'll always find a way to get to you": Technology use in adolescent romantic relationships and its role in dating violence and abuse. *Journal of Interpersonal Violence, 32*(14), 2083–2117. Available from https://doi.org/10.1177/0886260515590787.

Tong, S. T. (2013). Facebook use during relationship termination: Uncertainty reduction and surveillance. *Cyberpsychology, Behavior, and Social Networking* (16, pp. 788–793).

Tong, S. T., Van Der Heide, B., Langwell, L., & Walther, J. B. (2008). Too much of a good thing? The relationship between number of friends and interpersonal impressions on Facebook. *Journal of Computer-Mediated Communication, 13,* 531–549.

Utz, S., & Beukeboom, C. J. (2011). The role of social network sites in romantic relationships: Effects on jealousy and relationship happiness. *Journal of Computer-Mediated Communication, 16,* 511–527. Available from https://doi.org/10.1111/j.1083-6101.2011.01552.x.

Valenzuela, S., Halpern, D., & Katz, J. E. (2014). Social network sites, marriage well-being and divorce: Survey and state-level evidence from the United States. *Computers in Human Behavior, 36,* 94–101. Available from https://doi.org/10.1016/j.chb.2014.03.034.

White, G. L. (1981). Some correlates to romantic jealousy. *Journal of Personality, 49,* 129–145. Available from https://doi.org/10.1111/j.1467-6494.1981.tb00733.x.

Young, K. S. (2006). Online infidelity: Evaluation and treatment implications. *Journal of Couple and Relationship Therapy, 5,* 43–56.

THE DARK SIDE OF PROFESSIONAL SOCIAL MEDIA USE

Social Media Monitoring: A Cautionary View

INTRODUCTION

There is a general consensus in the field of marketing and communication that managers need reliable information in order to make better decisions. Traditional marketing has mostly relied on market research information, including secondary data (e.g., customer complaint reports) or primary data (e.g., consumer surveys). Studies show growth rates of market research revenues over the last years, indicating an increasing need for accurate and timely data. This also inspires companies to use new sources of data to learn about their markets.

With the rise of social media, and in particular the concept of social media marketing (Felix et al., 2017), there came another source of data: user-generated content (UGC) on social media channels. UGC is a general term that describes any form of content, ranging from simple "likes," short comments, and postings to detailed reports, audio files, pictures, videos, and other forms of media (Dhar & Chang, 2009; Kaplan & Haenlein, 2010). Since social media users produce a lot of UGC about a variety of different topics that are important to people, UGC often also includes information about brands (Mahrous, 2016).

Not surprisingly, the literature enthusiastically discusses the potential to apply certain data collection and analysis methods to distill relevant information from social media (King, Racherla, & Bush, 2014; Peters, Chen, Kaplan, Ognibeni, & Pauwels, 2013). Managers and scholars see numerous advantages in monitoring UGC, which has led to intense discussion of its benefits. However, in the literature there is a lack of critical perspective on social media monitoring and its current practice. Against this background, the following chapter provides a cautionary view of social media monitoring. However, this is not to say that social media monitoring is a bad approach that companies should avoid. On the contrary, the purpose of this chapter is to highlight potential limitations of this concept in order to (1) provide managers and scholars with a checklist to critically assess social media monitoring results, (2) stimulate future research to address these challenges, and (3) complement the literature with a closer look at the challenges of social media monitoring.

The structure of this chapter is as follows: first, we define social media monitoring and discuss how it differs from related concepts. Then we summarize many of the (presumed) advantages experts frequently discuss. In the main part of this chapter, we discuss certain limitations and challenges associated with social media monitoring. The chapter closes with a discussion of how managers can identify and overcome potential limitations.

SOCIAL MEDIA MONITORING: DEFINITION AND ADVANTAGES

Definition of Social Media Monitoring

"Social media monitoring" is defined as the systematic, continuous, and specific search, collection, processing, analysis, interpretation, and storage of managerially relevant social media content (typically UGC). The objective of social media monitoring is to give organizations a continuous overview of market trends in their own and related markets. Topics monitored relate not only to an organization itself but also to other relevant players, such as competitors or suppliers. However, social media monitoring (like social media marketing in general) is not limited to consumers or UGC. Organizations can monitor their employer brand (e.g., reviews on glassdoor.com), B2B companies can monitor consumers (e.g., a malting plant could monitor consumer discussions related to beer consumption), or political parties can monitor general trends. Finally, monitoring can cover content posted by other organizations in relevant markets (e.g., competitors), although the focus of this chapter is UGC.

A related approach is netnography, a concept also known as virtual ethnography, cyber-ethnography, or online ethnography. In general, netnography adapts traditional ethnographic research methods to the online context. Ethnographic consumer researchers typically study consumers in their natural settings (e.g., at home or in conversation) over a long period of time. Therefore sample sizes of ethnographic studies are usually small but contain a lot of deep, rich data that has been collected over time in order to build theories. Practically speaking, netnography researchers look for and analyze the in-depth content of Internet users, studying behavior (including uncovered meanings and values) through UGC.[1]

By contrast, social media monitoring typically focuses on a large amount of UGC in order to quantify insights (e.g., "How many people posted about our brand yesterday?") rather than explaining deep psychological meaning (e.g., "Which unmet fundamental human needs explain this behavior?").

Social media monitoring can contribute to a variety of disciplines, such as market research, social media marketing, or crisis communication.

---

[1]Note that the concept of netnography is much more complex than discussed in this chapter. The following publications (see the reference section) provide deeper insights into this highly relevant research approach: O'Donohoe (2010) and Kozinets (2002, 2017).

For example, as discussed in this chapter on collaborative brand attacks (i.e., user attacks on brands), monitoring can reduce the risk of being attacked by users and guide crisis communication managers. The focus of the present study, however, is monitoring as a source of market information.

Myths of Social Media Monitoring

Since social media monitoring is a highly interesting topic for many managers, there is a lot of hype about the benefits social media monitoring can provide. Some statements might even give the impression that social media monitoring is a blanket solution to any business problem. The following list provides an overview of "advantages" (which it turns out might actually be myths actually myths, as discussed later), which have been distilled from the intense debate on social media monitoring:

- Myth 1: Social media monitoring can generate reliable and objective key performance indicators (KPIs).
- Myth 2: Social media monitoring is not expensive, since many tools are free and no humans are needed for the data collection
- Myth 3: Social media monitoring can easily understand textual content and is thus able to generate reliable information.
- Myth 4: Social media monitoring can generate representative results.
- Myth 5: Social media monitoring can replace traditional and expensive market research.
- Myth 6: Social media monitoring can happen in real time.
- Myth 7: Social media monitoring can improve customer relationship management.
- Myth 8: Social media monitoring can protect companies from social media crises (collaborative brand attacks).
- Myth 9: Sentiment scores provide a reliable KPI to measure brand performance.

This list of myths is, of course, not exhaustive. In the following sections, we dive deeper into the methodology of social media monitoring. Based on that, we discuss how true these myths really are.

Quantifying User-Generated Content

A main objective of social media monitoring is the quantification of UGC so that managers can calculate KPIs, metrics (Töllinen & Karjaluoto, 2011). Often, UCG is qualitative in nature, for example, text, video, images, and so forth. In such cases, marketers need to find ways to quantify qualitative UCG in order to calculate KPIs (marketer-generated KPIs). In other situations, user behavior is already quantified (user-generated KPIs that count specific user activities). UGC can be described based on multiple dimensions (usually restricted to a certain time period; for an overview of metrics, see Peters et al., 2013). These include the following:

- Volume: The amount of UGC a brand receives in a certain time period.
- Valence: The sentiment or tonality of UGC, ranging from very negative via neutral to very positive.
- Variance: A measure of agreement between users, which describes how strongly the valence of brand-related UGC deviates from the average rating. For example, consider a brand with a neutral valence. In this case the variance would be low if most users wrote neutral postings about the brand. It would be high if half of the users rated it as very positive and the other half as very negative.
- Virality: The extent to which brand-related UGC spreads across different platforms or channels (Sterne, 2010). Common examples are the number of retweets, or how often a YouTube video is embedded elsewhere.

User-Generated Key Performance Indicators

User-generated KPIs are influenced directly by users' actions. Common examples are the number of followers, likes, comments, or shares a posting receives, or the number of times a video is viewed. These KPIs are considered more fact based and fairly objective, but a core challenge is to link these KPIs to specific objectives. For example, the number of postings that include a campaign-specific hashtag (e.g., #shareacoke) can be linked to the effectiveness of the "Share a Coke" campaign. Thus the correlation between ad spending and number of postings that include the hashtag #shareacoke can serve as an indicator (note: not as proof!) of ad effectiveness. Similarly, the number of likes a specific ad video receives (e.g., in relation to number of followers or reach of a posting) can serve as an indicator of attitude toward an ad.

Many organizations use these "hard facts" as criteria to assess their social media performance and see multiple advantages in such figures (e.g., that they are very objective, automatically trackable, and so forth). A subject managers often discuss is number of

Facebook likes or followers. However, multiple developments in the functionality of platforms (especially in their algorithms) and practices in the marketplace make these user-generated KPIs less effective. For example, even bad content can receive many likes if an algorithm classifies a posting as relevant and makes it accessible to many consumers.

Example: A recent trend includes "engagement groups" on social media platforms where users share likes. That is, a user posts a posting and asks members of an engagement group to click the like button of this posting. Algorithms can interpret many likes within a very short time period as an indicator of high quality content. Postings that are classified as high in quality are in turn made visible to larger audiences through the social media platform's algorithms, which might also lead to more likes (by chance).

Likewise, companies can promote postings (e.g., by paying money to Facebook), which generally leads to more likes. Therefore companies can put likes in relation to other measures, such as number of followers or reach of a posting (i.e., how many people saw a particular posting). However, this is not always possible. For example, when monitoring competitors, it is hard to interpret whether a competitor's posting has received a lot of likes because it is good or because it has been promoted to millions of users. Another common criticism of user-generated KPIs is the number of "bad followers" involved, that is, passive followers who do not follow a brand out of intrinsic motivation. For example, many companies try to motivate consumers to follow a brand in order to take part in a raffle, and others buy followers—strategies, that most experts would not recommend.

Marketer-Generated Key Performance Indicators

As discussed earlier, most UGC is qualitative in nature and therefore needs to be quantified before marketers can use it to calculate KPIs. A common approach to this is known as "content analysis" (Berelson, 1952). Content analysis is an established research strategy that, put simply, quantifies qualitative data (Kondracki, Wellman, & Amundson, 2002). For example, researchers have for decades analyzed how often particular topics or terms appear in newspaper articles, movies, and so forth, in order to describe and identify trends (Hurwitz et al., 2018).

Example: Social media user John posts the following about a recent restaurant visit:

> The food was great, the staff were friendly and prices were very reasonable. Clear recommendation! ★ ★ ★ ★ ★ (5/5 stars)

Social media user Mike posts the following about the same restaurant:

> My food was cold and we had to wait for hours, although the restaurant was empty. When we tried to ask staff what was going on, they were just rude and unfriendly. ★ ☆ ☆ ☆ ☆ (1/5 stars)

In this very simplified example a restaurant manager would have two postings to code. Since content analysis represents a "bundle" of specific approaches, scholars can analyze these two postings in different ways. A simple way would be to code each posting in terms of "positive" or "negative." In this case the first posting is clearly positive, and the second one clearly negative. The easiest approach would be to take the star rating (which would be a user-generated KPI) or to analyze the text. For a human, it is relatively easy to understand that the first posting is positive and the second negative. However, since strong brands receive a lot of buzz on social media, it might be more efficient to use automatic coding techniques, that is, software tools that collect, code, and analyze the data. Put simply, these tools look for words that are positive and negative. For example, John's post includes the words "great," "friendly," and "clear recommendation," whereas Mike's review contains predominantly negative words (e.g., "wait for hours," "unfriendly," and "rude").

A very basic content analysis approach would be to calculate a sentiment score. The core idea of sentiment scores is to put the number of positive reviews in relation to the number of negative reviews. In this case the sentiment score would be zero (50% positive − 50% negative = 0). However, it is important to note that different formulas for calculating sentiment scores exist.

More detailed analyses of user-generated data take a closer look at the content itself. For example, both users talk about the food and the staff, whereas only John talks about prices. For this kind of analysis, users need a detailed coding sheet in which they classify the content. Each topic (e.g., food) would be considered a variable (e.g., a column in a spreadsheet). Coders would then record whether the topic appears in a posting and, if so, whether the mention is positive or negative.

In theory, this looks like a simple approach. However, the reality is much more complex. To give some examples, some postings are neutral "EVERYTHING was OK!", whereas others might contain positive and negative content "the food was great, but the staff were unfriendly", so researchers need to specify and define their coding. In addition, some postings are very long and detailed, whereas others are short. For example, one might question whether a detailed posting with 500 words, which discusses multiple topics in detail, could be compared to a one-sentence posting. Finally, even when coding consumer online reviews in terms of "overall positive" or "overall negative" (which is a very simple and prestructured form of brand-related UGC), humans might have problems in interpreting the meaning of posts. For example, in a class project we developed a couple of years ago, we gave students some online reviews and asked them to code them. Then we asked them to compare their results with their neighbors. Surprisingly, only 60%–70% of the posts were coded identically by each pair of students. And it was easy to see what problems the students had:

1. unclear definitions of "positive" and "negative,"
2. unclear understanding of what users wanted to express in their short posts,
3. problems in coding posts that discussed both positive and negative aspects, and
4. other categories (e.g., neutral) were missing.

This provides anecdotal evidence for core problems of content analysis in practical applications: coders need clear instructions and definitions of categories. Second, in many specific situations, the meaning of a post cannot be understood based on the text alone. In some cases, for instance, the text of a post can only be understood together with the star ratings and uploaded images that accompany it. It is important to stress that UGC is a form of secondary data that was not created for the purpose of providing codable information to researchers. In many cases, UGC is a form of self-expression, excitement, or frustration, which is why many postings are so short. Third, there needs to be enough categories to code. Just positive and negative might not be enough (additional categories might be neutral, positive about aspect X, etc.).

Since scholars show a keen interest in assessing the reliability of content analysis, the literature provides some guidance on how coding reliability can be estimated. The most common forms are called intercoder reliability (the agreement between different coders) and intracoder

TABLE 6.1 Example Coding of 20 Postings by
Two Coders

Posting	Coder 1	Coder 2
1	N	P
2	N	N
3	P	P
4	P	P
5	P	P
6	P	P
7	P	P
8	P	P
9	P	P
10	P	P
11	P	P
12	P	P
13	N	N
14	P	P
15	P	P
16	P	P
17	N	N
18	P	P
19	P	P
20	N	N

N, Negative tonality; *P*, positive tonality.

reliability (if one person codes the same posting twice, does it lead to identical coding?). Over the years, many specific ways to calculate such reliability scores have developed.

Table 6.1 provides a fictitious example with a list of 20 different postings that two coders independently rated as positive (P) or negative (N).

In order to calculate intercoder reliability, some preliminary calculations are required. As shown in Table 6.2, the first step is to create a

TABLE 6.2 Preliminary Steps to Calculate Intercoder Reliability

		Coder 1			
		Positive	Negative	Σ	%
Coder 2	Positive	15 [a]	1 [b]	16	0.8
	Negative	0 [c]	4 [d]	4	0.2
	Σ	15	5	20 [n]	
	%	0.75	0.25		

table that shows how the two coders rated the postings. As shown, 15 of the 20 postings were rated as positive by both coders, 4 were rated as negative by both, and just 1 posting was rated differently (No. 1, which coder 1 rated as negative and coder 2 as positive). In other words, 19 out of 20 postings ($p_0 = 0.95$) were coded identically by both coders.

Qualitative researchers argue that a simple agreement score might not be the best approach, and therefore recommend coefficients that take into account the agreement between the reviewers by chance, that is, a baseline agreement.

In the next step, researchers calculate p_0 which, in this case, is $p_0 = 0.95$ and represents the observed proportional agreement between the two coders (i.e., the percentage of postings that both coders rated identically), thus

$$p_0 = \frac{a+d}{a+b+c+d} = \frac{a+d}{n}$$

In a further step, researchers calculate the probability of random agreement. The probability that both coders would rate a posting as positive is calculated as follows:

$$p_{positive} = \frac{a+b}{a+b+c+d} \cdot \frac{a+c}{a+b+c+d}$$

In this case, we find $p_{positive} = 0.60$ (one could also just multiply 0.75 by 0.80).

The same calculation is necessary to calculate the probability that both coders would rate a posting as negative, which in this case is $p_{negative} = 0.05$:

$$p_{negative} = \frac{c+d}{a+b+c+d} \cdot \frac{d+b}{a+b+c+d}$$

Thus the random agreement probability, that is, the probability that both coders agree as to whether a posting is positive or negative, is $p_c = 0.65$ and is calculated as follows:

$$p_c = p_{\text{positive}} + p_{\text{negative}}$$

Finally, researchers can calculate Cohen's kappa using the following formula:

$$\kappa = \frac{p_0 - p_c}{1 - p_c}$$

Or, in words

$$\kappa = \frac{\text{Observed agreement} - \text{agreement expected by chance alone}}{\text{Total potential agreement} - \text{agreement expected by chance alone}}$$

Note: Total potential agreement is usually 100%.

κ Values close to 1 indicate good intercoder reliability. The literature provides inconsistent recommendations about threshold values for κ. In this example, where both coders only disagreed in 1 out of 20 postings, $\kappa = 0.857$, the value is typically considered as good considered good. Especially when sample sizes are small, even small changes in the ratings can influence κ substantially. For example, if coder 2 had rated posting no. 2 as positive rather than negative, κ would decrease to $\kappa = 0.69$.

Readers might realize that the abovementioned example is artificial for several reasons. In reality, coders might include a neutral category, might have more nuanced measures for positive and negative (e.g., "The food was good" is not as positive as a post stating "The best food I've ever had!!!"), might code more than 20 postings, and probably would not be willing to calculate a coefficient manually. Fortunately, software tools such as SPSS can calculate intercoder reliability with very few clicks. In addition, more sophisticated kappas have been developed that can handle more than two manifestations (e.g., negative, neutral, and positive), weight disagreements (e.g., if coder 1 rates a posting as negative and coder 2 as neutral, the disagreement would be lower than if coder 2 rated the same posting as positive), continuous variables, or more than two coders. However, the basic principle of corrected agreement levels is similar across most intercoder reliability measures.

Intercoder reliability should play an important role in social media monitoring since it can identify problems in the definition of sentiment scores. If a company decides to code user postings manually, a second coder should at least code a random subsample of postings to assess intercoder reliability. Especially in the early stage of monitoring, having multiple coders can be helpful for the development of an effective coding strategy (which also includes training the coders). If companies use computer-aided coding tools, a promising approach to assessing the reliability of the tool could be to compare computer-coded postings with human-coded postings. This is particularly important since automatic coding tools might struggle with some general challenges, as discussed in the next section.

GENERAL LIMITATIONS OF SOCIAL MEDIA CONTENT ANALYSIS

Closed Networks

WhatsApp and other messaging services have risen in prominence in recent years. Therefore it is not surprising that many consumer discussions about brands happen in closed environments that researchers cannot easily access. Indeed, some studies suggest that consumers prefer closed environments in order to protect their privacy, sharing opinions only with people they know, and trust without being visible for employers or other parties with commercial interests.

Lack of Representativity

A lack of representativity is a challenge for almost all data collection methods, including standard methods such as surveys. Whenever certain respondents do not have the chance or are not willing to take part in surveys, or when some respondents are over-represented in surveys, results can be skewed and biased (Keeter, 2018; Rässler & Riphahn, 2006). When it comes to content analysis in social media, the following types of nonrepresentativity can have a crucial impact on results:

- Representativity of users
  Although the number of Internet users is increasing, there is still a large proportion of offliners (for country statistics, see https://www.internetworldstats.com). These are often very young or very old people, but also people from countries with legal or technological

barriers to the Internet, or people who intentionally decide not to be online. Their opinions cannot be captured through social media monitoring.

- Self-selection bias

    The probability of sharing a brand-related experience on social media is not equal for all people. In other words, some people are highly motivated to share every experience online, whereas others do not share any information online at all (Leung, 2009). Indeed, a majority of online users is very passive when it comes to online reviews. Informally, the social media research community has established the "90−9−1" rule (Priem & Hemminger, 2010; Van Mierlo, 2014), indicating that 90% of social media users are passive (lurkers), 9% somewhat active (contributors), and only 1% very active (super users). Heinonen (2011) argued that social media behaviors can range from consumption to participation to production of content, whereby the latter provides the richest information but is least prevalent. Research has widely replicated the finding that individual variables, such as personality, motivation, user popularity, or demographics, explain a substantial amount of variance in social media behaviors (Çiçek & Eren-Erdogmus, 2013; Goes, Lin, & Au Yeung, 2014; Quan-Haase & Young, 2010; Seidman, 2013; Sheldon, & Bryant, 2016). In other words, people of certain demographics or with certain psychographic characteristics are more or less likely to engage in specific UGC-related behaviors on social media.

- Topic bias

    In addition, there might be bias about the products people talk about. Generally speaking, strong consumer brands (e.g., Apple) and products that people frequently use (e.g., smartphones or cars) are referred to in many user conversations online. However, when it comes to low-involvement topics (e.g., toilet paper or salt), not as many users might share detailed experiences online. In the context of movies, Dellarocas, Gao, and Narayan (2010) showed that people are more likely to comment on niche products and successful products which many other users have already commented on. Moderately successful products thus receive less attention from social media users. Therefore some brands might struggle with very small numbers of postings to analyze: extreme opinions might be overrepresented (see the next bullet point) and sample sizes too small to calculate robust KPIs.

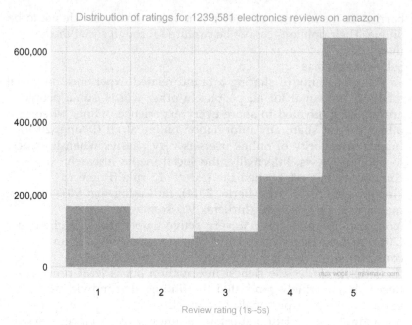

FIGURE 6.1   J-Function of online reviews. *Source: https://minimaxir.com/2014/06/reviewing-reviews/.*

- Extreme opinions (J-shaped functions)

   A common observation in online reviews is that very positive and very negative reviews are overrepresented (Hu, Zhang, & Pavlou, 2009). This phenomenon is called "J-function" (see Fig. 6.1) and has at least two possible explanations. First, users might exaggerate in reviews (e.g., because they are enthusiastic or frustrated while writing the review, want to impact the average rating, or, as suggested by Admati and Pfleiderer (2004), are overconfident). Second, "averagely happy" consumers are not highly motivated to share an average opinion with others (self-selection bias, as discussed earlier). This, however, means that a brand that has a lot of "moderately happy" consumers might (1) not receive enough reviews to get a large enough sample and/or (2) extreme values might lead to a false conclusion.
- Skewness due to bots and fake users

   In recent years, some dubious practices have been observed on social media. In particular, some companies have been inclined to spread fake reviews to promote their own brand or to harm competitors. Likewise, especially during elections, social bots spread "opinions" automatically. These fake opinions can easily give the impression that large numbers of users like (or dislike) a certain brand (including political parties). The literature provides some initial attempts to find algorithms to detect fakes (e.g., Akoglu, Chandy, & Faloutsos, 2013). And websites such as fakespot.com can help consumers to rate the credibility of online reviews.

In sum, there is a reasonable argument for scholars and managers to carefully assess the potential limitations that come from a lack of representativity. For example, a team of practitioners and scholars associated with the University of Boston conducted a survey in which they asked approximately 4000 consumers about nearly 100 brands across different dimensions. They enriched their dataset with manually coded sentiment scores. Surprisingly, "[t]here appears to be very little predictive power between how people appear to feel online and how consumers who have experiences with those brands rate them" (Panepinto, 2018). Very similar results are reported in a paper published by Fay and Larkin (2017). Finally, in an unpublished study, we compared employer brand ratings on the German "kununu" platform (similar to glassdoor.com) with employer brand attractiveness scores measured by a large-scale survey. We found very low correlations and an average of only ~4% shared variance between the two sources. This means that peaks or rapid changes in sentiment do not necessarily mean that "all" consumers changed their mind, it could also mean that a particular subset of users with a very strong opinion (e.g., they hate a campaign) generated a disproportionate volume of UGC.

POTENTIAL LIMITATIONS OF AUTOMATIC SOCIAL MEDIA CONTENT ANALYSIS

Due to the potentially large amount of brand-related UGC, many managers are interested in tools that automatically collect, analyze, and visualize UGC. Indeed, many free and commercial tools exist, which promise support in analyzing UGC. While automation has many advantages (especially in managing large amounts of data), users of these tools must know their limitations. This section, then, discusses some general limitations of monitoring tools. (It is not a general critique of all social media monitoring tools.)

Typos, Slang, and Context

The basic idea of automatic coding is that crawlers search for brand-related content and assess the tonality of words that are included. For example, the posting "The food was good" is identified as positive. A simple tool might assess the tonality of each word (The: no tonality; food: no tonality; was: no tonality; good: positive). A similar posting might be "the food wasn't that good." In this case a tool must understand that "wasn't that good" has a negative tonality, although it includes a positive word. Most tools can handle this nowadays.

For some consumers, writing social media postings is nothing special anymore. For example, proactive social media users may write online reviews or share their experiences with a restaurant while they are still eating. Therefore it is not surprising that many online reviews contain typos or slang. For example, a consumer eating at "John's BBQ house" might write "Johns Barbecue House" or "BBQ John." Many crawlers claim to be able to handle different spellings. However, consider a situation in which another user posts about a barbecue party at his friend John's house "having barbecue at John's house tonight!". Monitoring tools, then, need to be able to distinguish between different spellings, typos, and contexts (e.g., location). However, such information is not always accessible, and this might affect the results. For larger brands with a lot of UGC, misinterpretations can be considered general "noise" in the data.

Irony and Double Meaning

People sometimes say the opposite to what they really think (irony). In interpersonal situations, other people can usually decode the meaning of messages and detect irony. Some tools claim to handle irony effectively, but it's worth noting that even in some everyday conversations, detecting irony is challenging. Likewise, most coding tools analyze the words that surround a keyword (e.g., a brand name) to detect whether they have a positive tonality (e.g., great, good, amazing) or a negative tonality (e.g., bad, expensive, terrible). However, users sometimes use slang in which a word means the opposite of what it usually does (e.g., "great shit"; in this case, a monitoring tool would have to understand that the positive and negative words together do not mean "neutral," but something like "very good").

Nontextual Content

Among the strongest growing social media platforms are WhatsApp, Snapchat, and Instagram. Even on platforms such as Facebook, many users use memes (e.g., gifs) to express their opinion on certain topics. This, however, means that the amount of user-generated *text* decreases, and the amount of other forms of media increases. For researchers, this means that contemporary tools need to correctly understand additional forms of media (e.g., photos, videos, audio). As already discussed, the interpretation of text is challenging, but compared to other forms of media, text is relatively easy to "understand." For example, while it is technologically challenging enough for tools to identify brand logos in pictures, these tools also need to interpret images as intentionally or unintentionally included (e.g., a person holding a Coke can into the camera versus a person sitting at a fast food restaurant with a Coke ad in the background). In addition, interpreting the meaning of images is highly contextual. For example, consider the difference between a crushed can of Red Bull and a noncrushed one. Initially, one would argue that a crushed can indicates trash (=bad), and a noncrushed one indicates something positive (or at least neutral). Now take a look at the four Red Bull cans in Fig. 6.2. Of the two crushed cans the one at the bottom will

FIGURE 6.2   Red Bull cans (UGC). *UGC*, User-generated content. *Authors unknown.*

likely be associated with something positive (e.g., strength, energy, power), whereas the top one could be seen as trash (at least without knowing the context). Likewise, the added word "poison" is clearly negative, but it could be hard to detect by a tool because of the lack of contrast.

Unclear Identification of Brands

While it can be challenging to recognize and identify brands automatically in photos or videos, it can also be difficult in text. For example, some consumers use altered names for brands they do not like (e.g., "Fivebucks Coffee" instead of Starbucks Coffee to express their disliking of the high prices), as well as established abbreviations (e.g., "B-Dubs" for "Buffalo Wild Wings"). Researchers can solve this challenge by teaching tools additional spellings or terminology. Some tools even claim to learn such related terms automatically.

Lack of Transparency in Tools

Finally, it is worth noting that no research methodology is without its limitations. When researchers carry out quantitative surveys, for example, they are typically aware of the common limitations such as lack of depth or skewed sample distributions. While this chapter summarizes many of the potential weaknesses a tool can technically have, researchers need to be able to judge the validity of these tools. They therefore need access to transparent documentation of the relevant data collection methods, coding, and calculations. However, surprisingly few details are available for many tools, especially free ones. For example, the only such information that socialmention.com provides is on their sentiment score, described in their FAQ-section as follows: "Sentiment is the ratio of mentions that are generally positive to those that are generally negative." There is no information on how they assess a posting as being generally positive or negative. As an example, Fig. 6.3 shows the results from socialmention.com for "McDonalds" and "McDonald's." Initially, one would expect both sentiment scores to be very similar. But the results indicate 3:1 (positive:negative) for "McDonalds" versus 1:2 for "McDonald's." While such a free tool is, without doubt, an interesting starting point, contradictory or surprising findings as in this case might lead managers to question the explanatory power and validity of the conclusions.

39%	3:1	26%	1:2
Strength	Sentiment	Strength	Sentiment

11%	36%	5%	26%
Passion	Reach	Passion	Reach

2 min avg.per mention   2 min avg.per mention

Last mention 7 min ago   Last mention 7 min ago

71 Unique authors   38 Unique authors

48 Retweets   21 Retweets

Sentiment   Sentiment

Positive		13
Neutral		64
Negative		4

Positive		2
Neutral		34
Negative		4

FIGURE 6.3   McDonalds versus McDonald's (November 20, 2018).

DISCUSSION

As already mentioned, companies and scholars are both interested in the information contained in UGC on social media. While the literature has discussed many advantages of UGC, there are a number of shortcomings that researchers should keep in mind. At the beginning of this chapter, we presented a list of nine social media monitoring myths before discussing the potential limitations of social media monitoring. Table 6.3 lists these myths once again, together with relevant summaries of the topics discussed earlier.

A particular focus of this chapter is the idea that software can code UGC automatically. Indeed, there is a consensus that automation of social media monitoring is necessary, given the large volume of UGC that many brands receive. However, keeping the potential limitations of automatic coding in mind (which can, of course, vary between tools), managers and researchers should consider the following recommendations:

1. Cross-validate the findings
    As no research methodology is without limitations, researchers should compare the results of a specific monitoring tool with other

TABLE 6.3   Evaluation of the Social Media Monitoring Myths

Myth	Conclusion	Solutions
Social media monitoring can generate reliable and objective KPIs	Since many monitoring tools do not provide transparency on how to collect, code, and analyze data, KPIs are often not objective. In addition, KPIs can be influenced by external forces such as bots	Request detailed explanations of the standard KPIs from monitoring agencies Request raw data and try to reproduce the numbers Keep in mind that changes in platform algorithms can change the meaning of certain KPIs
Social media monitoring is not expensive, since many tools are free and no humans are needed for the data collection	There are many free social media monitoring tools available, but there is a substantial risk that the methodology is unclear or relevant features are missing. In addition, there might not be enough data available to allow automatic coding to provide reliable results	Social media monitoring requires budgets and skills Smaller firms or brands with less unique brand names might find it better to monitor social media manually
Social media monitoring can easily understand textual content and is thus able to generate reliable information	There are many issues with text interpretation, although providers often claim they can handle this. However, UGC is shifting toward other forms of content, such as images and videos. Monitoring tools need to understand texts and other forms of media, as well as their interplay (e.g., a photo of a broken smartphone and the text "Now that's quality!")	Ensure how the tool handles the challenges discussed already (e.g., irony) Find out how relevant nontextual content is. If it is relevant, consider using tools that can deal with such content
Social media monitoring can generate representative results	There are still substantial numbers of offliners. In addition, many studies show that the majority of UGC is produced by a small number of users, or primarily prevalent in selected industries. Finally, very positive and very	Do not interpret monitoring results as representative Focus on relative numbers. For example, "how many percent of postings that include our brand are positive?" and interpret it in relation to other benchmarks, such as "how has this number changed

(Continued)

TABLE 6.3 (Continued)

Myth	Conclusion	Solutions
	negative consumer reviews are usually overrepresented	compared to last month?" or "how are we performing compared to our competitors?"
Social media monitoring can replace traditional and expensive market research	Social media monitoring can complement, but not replace, traditional market research	Triangulate findings from different sources and research approaches (mixed methods). In addition, use findings from social media monitoring to improve traditional market research or to help interpret unexpected findings
Social media monitoring can happen in real time	Social media monitoring can happen in real time if no manual handling (e.g., coding, data cleaning) is necessary and if enough data is available (volume)	For large brands, real-time dashboards can give interesting insights into sentiment. Brands with less social media volume might have to accept delayed information
Social media monitoring can protect companies from social media crises (collaborative brand attacks)	Effective social media monitoring can reduce the risk of being attacked by users via social media, but it can't prevent a company from all forms of critique or attack	Keep an eye on what is being said about your brand on social media. In other words, conduct social media monitoring. However, in order to reduce the risks of social media attacks, you should also accept different "laws" of effective communication, as discussed in this chapter of the book
Sentiment scores provide a reliable KPI to measure brand performance	Empirical findings indicate that many sentiment scores are only weakly related to financial performance or other large-scale survey data	Generate KPIs that are specifically linked to a certain objective (e.g., percentage of postings that "will buy product X"), rather than general sentiment scores. Do not rely on sentiment scores as the only way to measure reputation or brand image

KPI, Key performance indicator; *UGC*, user-generated content.

tools or other data collection methods. For example, are the results in line with those from traditional market research or with reports from the customer service department? Do these findings correspond to feedback from the social media managers who interact with users on a daily basis? If not, use unexpected findings to generate hypotheses that can be tested in more detail using the methodology that is best for each situation.

2. Compare human versus automatic coding

   Tools should provide researchers with raw data, including information on how things were coded (e.g., as positive or negative). Researchers should take a random subsample and code it by hand. Ideally, there will be a high amount of overlap. In other words the researcher and the tool should agree. In addition, researchers should check how a given tool handles typos or alternative spellings of the brand name.

3. Focus on relative numbers

   Given the number of limitations, caution must be taken in the interpretation of absolute numbers. For example, claiming that a brand's sentiment score of " + 22 is good" can be problematic since the "real" value could be substantially higher or lower. However, there may be situations where it is appropriate to assume a certain level of "noise" in the data (such as a consistent margin of error). Then, researchers should focus their attention on two particular relative numbers: first, on numbers relative to time, as changes in sentiment over time are often more insightful. For example, if, after a campaign, a brand's sentiment score increases from +22 to +33, this could be an indicator (not causal proof!) that the campaign positively impacted the brand. Therefore sentiment scores should be seen as a continuous measurement approach of online reputation. Second, results relative to those of competitors are helpful. A score of +22 can be good if all competitors' scores are substantially lower. However, the same score can also be bad if all competitors' scores are much higher. This procedure requires a lot of data, although this should not be a major issue for large brands.

4. Develop relevant KPIs

   In order to measure information on social media, marketers should develop KPIs related to their objectives. For example, Nike's "Colin Kaepernick" advertising campaign resulted in a significant spike of negative sentiment online after the campaign started, but it shifted to positive after a few days. When Nike examined only tweets that included purchase-intent information (e.g., "going to buy" vs "won't buy"), the sentiment ratio was 5:1 (positive:negative), which was also reflected in actual sales numbers.[2] Thus managers should make sure that the things they measure (i.e., KPIs) are good indicators of what they want to measure (i.e., whether goals are being met). Using the Nike example, if the goal is to measure attitude toward the campaign, more traditional sentiment scores might be good. If your goal is to measure impact on sales, the ratio of buy versus not-buy comments might be better.

Social media monitoring does indeed have many advantages and can contribute to an organization's success - as correctly discussed in many managerial and academic articles. Thus, we agree that social media monitoring is, if correctly used and carefully interpreted, a good approach and also a "must have" for any organization. However, social media monitoring is not a blanket solution. Managers should see its insights as revealing just one part of the bigger picture. They should keep in mind the potential limitations of this tool and figure out ways to overcome them.

References

Admati, A. R., & Pfleiderer, P. (2004). Broadcasting opinions with an overconfident sender. *International Economic Review, 45*(2), 467–498.
Akoglu, L., Chandy, R., & Faloutsos, C. (2013). Opinion fraud detection in online reviews by network effects. *ICWSM, 13*, 2–11.
Berelson, B. (1952). *Content analysis in communication research.* New York, NY, US: Free Press. Available from https://www.amazon.de/Handbook-Qualitative-Business-Management-Research/dp/1473926629.
Çiçek, M., & Eren-Erdogmus, I. (2013). Social media marketing: Exploring the user typology in Turkey. *International Journal of Technology Marketing, 8*(3), 254–271.
Dellarocas, C., Gao, G., & Narayan, R. (2010). Are consumers more likely to contribute online reviews for hit or niche products? *Journal of Management Information Systems, 27* (2), 127–158.
Dhar, V., & Chang, E. A. (2009). Does chatter matter? The impact of user-generated content on music sales. *Journal of Interactive Marketing, 23*(4), 300–307.
Fay, B., & Larkin, R. (2017). Why online word-of-mouth measures cannot predict brand outcomes offline: Volume, sentiment, sharing, and influence metrics yield scant online–offline WOM correlations. *Journal of Advertising Research, 57*(2), 132–143.
Felix, R., Rauschnabel, P. A., & Hinsch, C. (2017). Elements of strategic social media marketing: A holistic framework. *Journal of Business Research, 70*, 118–126.
Goes, P. B., Lin, M., & Au Yeung, C. M. (2014). "Popularity effect" in user-generated content: Evidence from online product reviews. *Information Systems Research, 25*(2), 222–238.

[2]More details on this case study are presented in Panepinto (2018), where from this example is taken, and Snah (2018).

Heinonen, Kristina (2011). Consumer activity in social media: Managerial approaches to consumers' social media behavior. *Journal of Consumer Behaviour, 10* (6), 356–364.

Hu, N., Zhang, J., & Pavlou, P. A. (2009). Overcoming the J-shaped distribution of product reviews. *Communications of the ACM, 52*(10), 144–147.

Hurwitz, L. B., Alvarez, A. L., Lauricella, A. R., Rousse, T. H., Montague, H., & Wartella, E. (2018). Content analysis across new media platforms: Methodological considerations for capturing media-rich data. *New Media & Society, 20*(2), 532–548.

Kaplan, A. M., & Haenlein, M. (2010). Users of the world, unite! The challenges and opportunities of Social Media. *Business Horizons, 53*(1), 59–68.

Keeter, S. (2018). *The impact of survey non-response on survey accuracy. The Palgrave Handbook of Survey Research* (pp. 373–381). Cham, Switzerland: Palgrave Macmillan.

King, R. A., Racherla, P., & Bush, V. D. (2014). What we know and don't know about online word-of-mouth: A review and synthesis of the literature. *Journal of Interactive Marketing, 28*(3), 167–183.

Kondracki, N. L., Wellman, N. S., & Amundson, D. R. (2002). Content analysis: Review of methods and their applications in nutrition education. *Journal of Nutrition Education and Behavior, 34*(4), 224–230.

Kozinets, R. V. (2002). The field behind the screen: Using netnography for marketing research in online communities. *Journal of Marketing Research, 39*(1), 61–72.

Kozinets, R. V. (2017). Netnography for management and business research. In *The SAGE handbook of qualitative business and management research methods: Methods and challenges* (p. 384).

Leung, L. (2009). User-generated content on the internet: An examination of gratifications, civic engagement and psychological empowerment. *New Media & Society, 11*(8), 1327–1347.

Mahrous, A. A. (2016). Implications of the use of social media for pre-purchase information searches for automobiles. *International Journal of Technology Marketing, 11*(3), 254–275.

O'Donohoe, S. (2010). *Netnography: Doing ethnographic research online.*

Panepinto, J. *Brands shouldn't believe everything they read about themselves online.* (2018). <https://hbr.org/2018/10/brands-shouldnt-believe-everything-they-read-about-themselves-online>.

Peters, K., Chen, Y., Kaplan, A. M., Ognibeni, B., & Pauwels, K. (2013). Social media metrics—A framework and guidelines for managing social media. *Journal of Interactive Marketing, 27*(4), 281–298.

Priem, J., & Hemminger, B. H. (2010). Scientometrics 2.0: New metrics of scholarly impact on the social Web. *First Monday, 15*(7).

Quan-Haase, A., & Young, A. L. (2010). Uses and gratifications of social media: A comparison of Facebook and instant messaging. *Bulletin of Science, Technology & Society, 30*(5), 350–361.

Rässler, S., & Riphahn, R. T. (2006). Survey item nonresponse and its treatment. *Allgemeines Statistisches Archiv, 90*(1), 217–232.

Seidman, G. (2013). Self-presentation and belonging on Facebook: How personality influences social media use and motivations. *Personality and Individual Differences, 54*(3), 402–407.

Sheldon, P., & Bryant, K. (2016). Instagram: Motives for its use and relationship to narcissism and contextual age. *Computers in Human Behavior, 58*, 89–97.

Snah, A. *Nike seizes controversy by the bullish horns.* (2018). <https://www.forbes.com/sites/alapshah/2018/09/12/a-social-media-and-sentiment-analysis-of-nike-what-does-it-mean-for-future-purchase-intent> Retrieved 15.11.18.

Sterne, J. (2010). *Social media metrics: How to measure and optimize your marketing investment.* John Wiley & Sons.

Töllinen, A., & Karjaluoto, H. (2011). Marketing communication metrics for social media. *International Journal of Technology Marketing, 6,* 316–330.

Van Mierlo, T. (2014). The 1% rule in four digital health social networks: An observational study. *Journal of Medical Internet Research, 16*(2), e33.

II. THE DARK SIDE OF PROFESSIONAL SOCIAL MEDIA USE

Online Firestorms: Collaborative Brand Attacks

INTRODUCTION

With the increasing popularity of social media, organizations have become interested in making use of the potential advantages that these new platforms offer (Felix, Rauschnabel, & Hinsch, 2017; Kaplan, & Haenlein, 2010). Indeed, both case studies (e.g., Dholakia & Durham, 2010) and academic research (Kim & Ko, 2012) have provided evidence that the use of social media has multiple advantages for organizations, such as positive effects on sales, reputation, recruiting, customer service, and so forth. However, managing brands[1] on social media is a complex endeavor. As metaphorically described by Hennig-Thurau, Hofacker, and Bloching (2013, pp. 237–238):

> Traditional marketing resembles bowling: A firm uses its marketing instruments (the ball) to reach and influence consumers (the pins). Mass media (the bowling alley) function as mediators for marketing content; these media have to be carefully attended to because they can also influence the effectiveness of marketing actions. Social media change the picture—marketing is now better characterized as a pinball game (Hennig-Thurau et al., 2010). The pinball machine comprises the environment in which, as in the bowling metaphor, marketing instruments (the balls) are used to reach consumers (the various targets of the machine—bumpers, kickers, and slingshots).

Managers have to accept this democratization of marketing practices and understand that many of the established management practices are not effective anymore (Asmussen, Harridge-March, Occhiocupo, & Farquhar, 2013; Divol, Edelman, & Sarrazin, 2012; Labrecque, vor dem Esche, Mathwick, Novak, & Hofacker, 2013). For example, in the presocial media era, managers could easily withdraw ineffective TV spots or billboard campaigns, and it was unlikely that consumers would create and distribute their own branded content. Nowadays, it is not uncommon for consumers to create branded content, alter branded content, or spread marketing messages on their own. While this can have many positive effects—in particular, more reach and more trustworthy messages—it can easily translate into negative word of mouth (WOM) (Relling, Schnittka, Sattler, & Johnen, 2016) or, in the worst case, into user attacks on companies, a new form of brand crises.

The aim of this chapter is to outline and discuss *collaborative brand attacks* (CBAs) as a social media–specific brand crisis and to compare them with traditional brand crises.[2] Based on that, this chapter will then present multiple prevention and reaction strategies and conclude with a checklist that managers can use to manage their social media reputation.

---

[1]The term brand, in this book, covers a variety of entities such as companies, consumer brands, people brands, place brands, NGO brands, and so forth.

[2]This chapter represents an applied and updated summary of Rauschnabel, Kammerlander, and Ivens (2016), published in the *Journal of Marketing Theory and Practice*.

SOCIAL MEDIA MARKETING

Broadly speaking, when marketers make use of social media, they often speak of "social media marketing." Early definitions of social media marketing had a narrow focus on marketing and advertising practices via social media to reach customers. Recently, Felix et al. (2017) have chosen a holistic approach and, based on multiple interviews, have defined social media marketing as "an interdisciplinary and cross-functional concept that uses social media (often in combination with other communications channels) to achieve organizational goals by creating value for stakeholders." This definition shows that organizations can achieve multiple goals (e.g., profit, reputation, market information through monitoring) across multiple stakeholders (e.g., customers, employees, public) with, or with the help of, social media. This complexity often affects multiple other departments besides marketing, such as human resources (since employees also share content online, or search for jobs through social media; see Sivertzen, Nilsen, & Olafsen, 2013), IT (since new platforms are required), customer relationship marketing (since new customer contacts need to be integrated into existing systems), public relations, and so forth. Thus effective social media marketing requires cross-functional collaboration in order to manage social media coherently. These complexities become amplified since, as we have discussed, Internet users have a lot of power—even control—over a brand and its reputation (Hennig-Thurau et al., 2010). One particularly crucial topic for managers is negative user-generated content (UGC), which, in the worst case, can turn into a new form of brand crisis (CBA, synonym: online firestorm, or, especially in German speaking countries, "shitstorm").

SOCIAL MEDIA CRISES: COLLABORATIVE BRAND ATTACKS

Exit, Loyalty, Voice: Three Basic Strategies of Unsatisfied Customers

Consumers' options in the "analog days" were quite limited. An unhappy customer had three basic options: "exit," "loyalty," and "voice":

1. The "exit" option describes the situation where an unhappy customer ends a relationship with a firm. In practice, this means that he or she stops buying products or services. As a consequence, a firm loses one

specific customer which, for most companies, is, financially speaking, not very dramatic.

2. The "loyalty" option refers to the fact that some unhappy consumers just accept their unhappiness and stay loyal. Reasons include, but are not limited to, a lack of alternatives, or convenience.

3. Finally, the "voice" option allows users to complain to a company, for example, in the hope of changing its behavior, showing goodwill, and so forth. "Voice" also covers negative WOM, which means that a customer shares his or her negative experiences with peers. Traditionally, negative WOM was limited to a small number of peers offline. The only powerful entities that could change an organization's behavior were mass media, for example, by covering a particular instance of organizational misbehavior over and over again. With social media, consumers' options have increased. For example, prior to any purchase decisions, many consumers research online reviews and other opinions and thus make better informed decisions. In addition, "voice" is not just limited to a person's peers. Every social media user can share any opinion online and thus make it accessible to millions of other users. This, of course, is not per se a downside of social media. On the contrary an increase of power for people and more information and transparency for decision-making are positive consequences of social media that "good organizations" typically do not have to worry about. Indeed, many happy customers share their experiences via social media, follow brands, share positive brand-related content, or defend a brand against criticism online. However, these mechanisms also have a downside for organizations, even for those that typically would not have to worry: unpredictable user attacks on their brand, as discussed in the following sections.

Unpredictable user attacks represent a fourth option—in addition to exit, voice, and loyalty—that people (and not just actual customers) have (Rauschnabel et al., 2016): *Attack*. These user attacks on brands through social media represent a novel form of communication crises that managers must deal with. In the next section, we will first provide a brief overview of traditional communication crises, before presenting a detailed definition of "CBAs" in social media, as well as their similarities to and differences from traditional brand crises.

Communication Crises and Collaborative Brand Attacks

Traditional Communication Crises

For decades, communication and marketing scholars and managers alike have had a keen interest in understanding communication crises (e.g., Coombs, 2007; Liu, Austin, & Jin, 2011). Simply speaking, most traditional communication crises resulted from mistakes by top management (e.g., child labor), accidents, disasters, and so forth. Many scholars argue that the severity of a crisis depends on the attribution of fault (Coombs & Holladay, 1996; Schwarz, 2012). For example, the attribution level is typically high if managers engage intentionally in ecologically damaging behavior and is low in case of an earthquake that is out of an organization's control. Typically, journalists identify a crisis or are among the first to cover it. Therefore mass media play an important role in how crisis information affects an organization's reputation among the public. Research has also shown that organizations with an unfavorable crisis history suffer more from a new crisis than similar organizations with a clear crisis history (Coombs, 2004). However, in traditional crises, communication managers would typically have had enough time—at least few days—to develop response strategies (Coombs, 2007; Coombs & Holladay, 2014; Rauschnabel et al., 2016). Also, multiple theories and frameworks provide guidance about possible reaction strategies. One of these possible strategies, for example, is to scale down communication and to wait until a crisis is over. Other strategies even encompass more aggressive responses, such as issuing a counter statement to the media.

Shell, for example, suffered a brand crisis in 1995. The company wanted to dispose of a decommissioned floating oil storage facility in the Atlantic rather than recycling the materials (i.e., high attribution). These plans were leaked to Greenpeace, which raised concerns. With the help of journalists, Greenpeace activists occupied the platform and mounted a media campaign against Shell, including a boycott of Shell products.

Nowadays many "traditional crises" spill over to social media and prompt users to create negative UGC. For example, when BP's oil platform Deepwater Horizon was leaking in 2010, traditional mass media extensively covered the event. Later, social media users altered brand logos (e.g., by adding an oil film to BP's logo), also motivated by a Greenpeace appeal to redesign the logo. Many of these altered logos are still available on a Greenpeace FLICKR channel; Fig. 7.1 shows two examples.

"Save the future, by saving today"

FIGURE 7.1   Altered BP logos. *Source: https://www.flickr.com/photos/greenpeaceuk/sets/ 72157623796911855/ (authors: unknown).*

Collaborative Brand Attacks

Broadly speaking, the word "attack" refers to the observation that users (and not just customers) create and share antibrand content online in order to harm a company. What the literature calls "online firestorms", "shitstorm", or "CBAs" is defined as "joint, event-induced, dynamic, and public attacks from a large number of Internet users via social media platforms on an organization, in order to harm it and/or to force it to change its behavior." We will now describe the core characteristics of CBAs, according to Rauschnabel et al. (2016), in detail.

"Event-induced and dynamic" is a characteristic that indicates that CBAs do not develop slowly over time or because of a company's general practice or philosophy (e.g., an organization promoting certain political views or a company that is known for price dumping). CBAs are typically induced by a *specific* event or action (e.g., a campaign, a leaked video, or a specific customer review) and start on a social media site. Many CBAs develop and grow dynamically within a very short time period in an uncontrolled way, in line with the mechanisms described in the "pinball metaphor." Most CBAs spread to other social media sites and may even be taken up by journalists from traditional mass media. Often, the initial purpose of the initiator is not to attack or harm the target organization. For example, sometimes a simple customer review containing a complaint will trigger a CBA, but subsequent collaborators in the CBA might intentionally attack and harm a brand.

In most CBAs a large number of users with varying degrees of activity participate jointly and collaboratively in the attack against an organization (Johnen, Jungblut, & Ziegele, 2018). These CBA-related activities can range from very passive behaviors (e.g., reading comments) to moderate behaviors (e.g., "liking" or "commenting" on CBA-related content) to very active "prosuming" (producing and consuming) behaviors which include the creation of original CBA-related content (e.g., antibrand videos).

Finally, it is worth noting that CBAs are public and hostile. This is an important characteristic because CBA-related UGC often stays online and thus accessible to other users years after a CBA. For example, if a large number of users "punish" a brand by writing thousands of negative reviews on an opinion platform (e.g., one-star reviews), the average rating of a firm will likely never recover from that, and this will impact purchase decisions of users for years following a CBA. In addition, search engines might still present CBA-related content at the top of the results list when consumers search for company-related information.

Research (e.g., Rauschnabel et al., 2016) has identified three broad categories that, isolated or in combination, can trigger CBAs:

1. Unethical behavior of an organization (social, ecological, legal, or political issues)
2. Problems in the core business (e.g., product-related problems, issues in customer service)
3. Unprofessional (social media) communication (e.g., lack of transparency in decision-making, unprofessional content, unfair statements)

These triggers do not always lead to CBAs, but several factors exist that increase the likelihood and strength of CBAs. For example, in situations where NGOs (e.g., Greenpeace) or informal communities (e.g., supporters of a person involved in a CBA) get involved, CBAs can gain momentum. Likewise, when the CBA initiators create appealing content (e.g., funny antibrand videos), other social media users are motivated to share this content and to create their own CBA content (Alexandrov, Lilly, & Babakus, 2013; Johnen et al., 2018). Finally, the momentum of CBAs can increase in situations where companies react wrongly (e.g., by ignoring or censoring CBA-related content, or by abusing their power in another way) or too late (e.g., several days later).

For companies, it is important to react quickly and correctly. If managers apply the "old laws of communication," they often assume that they have enough time to develop a well-planned reaction strategy. However, CBAs require a fast reaction. For example, Vodafone was the victim of a CBA which gained momentum because their social media team did not react to a polarizing Facebook posting that criticized their customer service on the weekend. Users felt they were being ignored, which intensified the CBA. Other firms, such as Nestlé, tried to survive a CBA by legal action. In this particular case, users had changed the "KitKat"-Logo to "Killer" (because they accused Nestlé of destroying the natural environment of orangutans), and Nestlé tried to sue users citing trademark violations. As a consequence, more users were motivated to spread the altered logos across multiple platforms from anonymous accounts. Likewise, whereas objective discussions with traditional media as well as counter-statements are sometimes effective reaction strategies for traditional communication crises, they are not a very effective strategy for CBAs. In these cases, many users perceive justifications as unethical and a provocation. Generally speaking, a combination of apologizing and changing behavior is the most effective reaction strategy to overcome CBAs. In some cases, especially among smaller companies, managers have applied a strategy termed "content bumping." This strategy may be effective in situations where the peak of a CBA is already over, but CBA-related content is still available online and easily accessible via search engines. Companies will then create a lot of new search-engine optimized, brand-related content with the intention that the CBA-related content to be "bumped" away from the top results on search engines.

Table 7.1 summarizes the core triggers, characteristics, strategies, and consequences of CBAs. In addition, the table provides a comparison to traditional communication crises.

TABLE 7.1 Traditional Communication Crises Versus Collaborative Brand Attacks (CBAs) (Online Firestorms)

	Traditional Crises	CBAs
Definition	"A crisis is a sudden and unexpected event that threatens to disrupt an organization's operations and poses both a financial and a reputational threat" (Coombs, 2007, p. 164)	Joint, event-induced, dynamic, and public attacks from a large number of Internet users via social media platforms on an organization, in order to harm it and/or to force it to change its behavior
Synonyms	Communication crisis, brand crisis, reputation crisis	Online firestorm, social media shitstorm

(Continued)

TABLE 7.1   (Continued)

	Traditional Crises	CBAs
Triggers/root causes	Corporate misbehavior (often by top management) Technical errors (e.g., product recalls) Natural disasters, etc.	Unethical behavior Problems in the core business (including on a lower level) Communication issues (including tactical issues such as a wrong wording in a single posting)
Main content creators	Mass media (journalists)	Social media users
Role of social media	Can become relevant after mass media coverage	CBAs develop in social media
Role of traditional media	Traditional crisis typically spread through traditional media	CBAs sometime spill over to traditional media
Crisis responsibility	Anywhere between low and high	Perceived as (very) high by consumers
Consequences	Loss of reputation	Loss of reputation (especially online)
Media tonality	Rather objective owing to codices	Rather subjective (even angry, insulting, threatening, etc.)
Time to react	Typically a few days	Often less than a few hours
Response strategies	Primary strategies: <ul><li>Attack the accuser: The crisis manager confronts the person or group claiming something to be wrong with the organization</li><li>Denial: The crisis manager asserts that there is no crisis</li><li>Scapegoat: The crisis manager blames some person or group outside the organization for the crisis</li><li>Excuse: The crisis manager minimizes organizational responsibility by denying intent to do harm and/or claiming inability to control the events that triggered the crisis</li></ul>	Because CBAs are so fast and dynamic, there are no primary and secondary response strategies <ul><li>Change behavior: The organization changes behavior (e.g., reverses decisions communicated, or changes the company's behavior)</li><li>Counter-statement: The organization states that their behavior was correct, or misunderstood by CBA participants</li><li>Appeasement: Users are placated</li><li>Ignoring: The organization ignores the attack</li><li>Bumping content: The company tries to avoid content by buying</li></ul>

(Continued)

TABLE 7.1   (Continued)

	Traditional Crises	CBAs
	• Justification: The crisis manager minimizes the perceived damage caused by the crisis • Compensation: The crisis manager offers money or other gifts to victims • Apology: The crisis manager indicates that the organization takes full responsibility for the crisis and asks stakeholders for forgiveness Secondary strategies: • Reminder: Crisis managers tell stakeholders about the past good works of the organization • Integration: Crisis managers praise stakeholders and/or remind them of past good works of the organization • Victimhood: Crisis managers remind stakeholders that the organization is a victim of the crisis, too.	up platforms (and then changing it through positive content) or bump the CBA in search engines by placing a lot of new content • Censoring/legal steps: The organization deletes negative UGC Note: Censoring/legal steps, counter-statement, and ignoring are strategies that—in most cases—even bring additional momentum to a CBA. These strategies thus represent only possible (and not recommended) strategies
Consequences	Loss of reputation Financial damage	Loss of reputation Financial damage

UGC, User-generated content.

Taken from Rauschnabel, P. A., Kammerlander, N., & Ivens, B. S. (2016). Collaborative brand attacks in social media: exploring the antecedents, characteristics, and consequences of a new form of brand crises. Journal of Marketing Theory and Practice, 24(4), 381–410; Coombs, W. T. (2007). Ongoing crisis communication. Planning, managing, and responding. Los Angeles, CA: Sage Publications; Felix, R., Rauschnabel, P. A., & Hinsch, C. (2017). Elements of strategic social media marketing: A holistic framework. Journal of Business Research, 70, 118–126; Hennig-Thurau, T., Hofacker, C. F., & Bloching, B. (2013). Marketing the pinball way: Understanding how social media change the generation of value for consumers and companies. Journal of Interactive Marketing, 27(4), 237–241; East, R., Hammond, K., & Lomax, W. (2008). Measuring the impact of positive and negative word of mouth on brand purchase probability. International Journal of Research in Marketing, 25(3), 215–224 (East, Hammond, & Lomax, 2008); Li, C., & Bernoff, J. (2011). Groundswell: Winning in a world transformed by social technologies. Harvard Business Press (Li & Bernoff, 2011); Johnen, M., Jungblut, M., & Ziegele, M. (2018). The digital outcry: What incites participation behavior in an online firestorm? New Media & Society, 20(9), 3140–3160 (Johnen et al., 2018); Hansen, N., Kupfer, A. K., & Hennig-Thurau, T. (2018). Brand crises in the digital age: The short-and long-term effects of social media firestorms on consumers and brands. International Journal of Research in Marketing, 35, 557–574 (Hansen, Kupfer, & Hennig-Thurau, 2018); Kristal, S., Baumgarth, C., & Henseler, J. (2018). "Brand play" versus "Brand attack": The subversion of brand meaning in non-collaborative co-creation by professional artists and consumer activists. Journal of Product & Brand Management, 27(3), 334–347 (Kristal, Baumgarth, & Henseler, 2018).

Union Street Guest House

Home | About Us | Rooms | Lobby/Lounge

Gym | Things to Do | Rates & Policies

Amenities | Dining | Events & Weddings

Check Availability | Directions | Contact Us

new) If your guests are looking for a Marriott type hotel
they may not like it here.
Therefore: If you have booked the Inn for a wedding or
other type of event anywhere in the region and given us
a deposit of any kind for guests to stay at USGH there
will be a $500 fine that will be deducted from your
deposit for every negative review of USGH placed on
any internet site by anyone in your party and/or attending
your wedding or event if you stay here to attend a
wedding anywhere in the area and leave us a negative
review on any internet site you agree to a $500. fine for
each negative review. (Please NOTE we will not charge
this fee &/or will refund this fee once the review is taken
down). Also, please note that we only request this of
wedding parties and for the reasons explained above.

Events & Weddings

HOME | ABOUT US | ROOMS | THINGS TO DO | DIRECTIONS | RATES & POLICIES | AMENITIES | DINING | EVENTS & WEDDINGS | RESERVATIONS | CONTACT US

FIGURE 7.2   Union Street Guest House. *Source: https://www.crmbuyer.com/story/80837. html.*

EXAMPLE: UNION STREET GUEST HOUSE

Although the first CBAs happened in the early 2000s, there are still many recent examples that could have been avoided through a better understanding of social media and its "dark side." For example, in 2014, a hotel in New York (Union Street Guest House) posted a Facebook posting in which they threatened users with a $500 fine for negative reviews (see Fig. 7.2).

Not surprisingly, users complained because they perceived this policy as highly unethical. Once traditional media became aware of the discussion and covered it through their channels, even more people joined the attack. As a consequence, users posted thousands of negative reviews across multiple platforms within a few days. Most of these users were probably not actual customers but just users who felt provoked and motivated to protect freedom of speech. Many of these reviews included polarizing and probably exaggerated statements about and photos of the hotel. In addition, a majority of users complained

Tomothy P.
Eden Prairie, MN
2 friends
13 reviews
93 photos

Share review

Embed review

Compliment

Send message

Follow Tomothy P.

9/3/2017

This is the 7th time I had to write this review on this deplorable company. Stop paying to make your image better, stop charging LOYAL customers $500 for not agreeing with your terrible and unethical business practices. Union House should be renamed "Screw you Because We have Your Credit Card information and we're going to charge you $500 multiple times just to spite you." Horrible company, even worst service, and to top it off ... Extremely bad management.

Jeff K. and 20 others voted for this review

Useful 20   Funny 3   Cool 3

FIGURE 7.3   CBA-related content. *CBA*, Collaborative brand attacks. *Source: https:// www.yelp.com/biz/union-street-guest-house-hudson.*

about this "philosophy" of banning criticism. After approximately 3000 negative reviews—much too late—the hotel apologized. However, the reviews stayed online, and as research has shown, reviews are powerful in influencing consumer behavior (Zhang, Craciun, & Shin, 2010). Shortly after the postings, the hotel closed. An example review is presented in Fig. 7.3.

COLLABORATIVE BRAND ATTACKS AND THE DARK SIDE OF SOCIAL MEDIA

Consumer power—the possibility to attack organizations—gives people a tremendous amount of influence. While power is not per se something negative, it can be used in a "dark" way. For example, whenever a consumer is unhappy with a product, he or she might perceive this as unethical behavior of an organization and threaten to launch a CBA, create antibrand UGC, and so forth. Since many organizations see the risk of CBAs, yet lack profound knowledge, users can instrumentalize these fears and threaten to produce negative reviews, antibrand videos, and so forth.

To a certain extent, organizations' fears are justified. For example, research has shown that even minimal actions—that is, a posting that has been written ambiguously—may be perceived as unethical and trigger CBAs with tremendous consequences for an organization's reputation and market performance. For example, INGDiba, a European bank, became the victim of a CBA because they showed Dirk Nowitzky, a German basketball player, eating a sausage in a TV ad. A group of "patriotic vegetarians" perceived this as a means of downplaying the killing of animals and initiated a CBA. Without doubt, traditional crisis theories would typically not assume that eating a sausage in an ad might trigger a crisis.

While it is unlikely that a company could eliminate all risk of falling victim to a CBA, they can at least reduce the risk. Table 7.2 summarizes some general prevention strategies.

TABLE 7.2 Checklist: Preventing Collaborative Brand Attacks (CBAs)

Prevention Strategy	Explanation
Continuous monitoring of social media content	The earlier CBAs are identified, the better an organization can react. Ideally, companies can even avoid a CBA by performing specific actions before negative content translates into a CBA
	For example, when United Airlines became the victim of a CBA (the "United Breaks Guitars" video), it took more than 1 week for their communications department to become aware of the video. See also Chapter 6 in this book on Social Media Monitoring: A Cautionary View
Pretesting of content	Slight changes in the wording of social media postings can prevent false interpretation of postings. Pretesting content can reduce the risk of misinterpretations
Educating employees	Employees who are aware of the risks of social media are less likely to use social media in a way that could trigger CBAs
	For example, Domino's Pizza fell victim to a CBA that was triggered by employees. These employees recorded themselves doing disgusting things with food, which they then shared via social media. Employees who are aware of the consequences of posting brand-related content on the Internet may be more responsible in their work-related social media use. In addition, social-media competent employees protect brands in antibrand discussions and report critical content to the social media managers of a company

(Continued)

TABLE 7.2   (Continued)

Prevention Strategy	Explanation
Communication on equal terms	If managers communicate with their users on equal terms without being arrogant, reactions may also be friendlier. Managers should not delete content (unless there are legal reasons to do so) and react timely and honestly to criticism
Build a strong community	A strong community of loyal users may defend a brand more authentically than the brand itself. This can appease (and ideally stop) a CBA in its early stages. However, building up and managing a strong community is a challenging endeavor
Redefine responsibilities and competencies	More departments have direct contact with stakeholders. Therefore they need to be trained in communication and must be aware of the social media strategy. For example, many marketing managers are not trained in personal interaction with consumers

Adapted from Rauschnabel, P. A., Kammerlander, N., & Ivens, B. S. (2016). Collaborative brand attacks in social media: exploring the antecedents, characteristics, and consequences of a new form of brand crises. Journal of Marketing Theory and Practice, 24(4), 381–410.

DISCUSSION

In this chapter, we discussed a new form of brand crises based on previous work by Rauschnabel et al. (2016): CBAs. CBAs can be a major threat to companies and require new strategies. Managers must accept their loss of power and adjust their well-established marketing and communication practices. For example, when consumers complain at night or on the weekend, they expect an immediate reaction. This means that social media managers technically have a 24/7 job, which might lead to additional conflicts (e.g., work–life balance, impact on their family lives). In addition, they need to have real-time knowledge of brand-related topics across multiple platforms, need internal collaboration, have to engage in discussions with unhappy (maybe even angry) users, and still stay professional. Another important aspect is that social media can also influence firms that are not present on social media. That is, even companies that proactively decide against the use of their own social media channels can be attacked via social media. In other words, even these companies should have an eye on social media. While social media has multiple advantages, and many books, chapters, and research papers shed light on how organizations should act in order to maximize the bright side of social media (e.g., Avery, Lariscy, Kim, & Hocke, 2010; Brown, Barry, Dacin, & Gunst, 2005; Felix et al., 2017), there is also a dark side. Therefore this chapter does not argue that social media or social media marketing are "bad." This chapter complements the predominantly "optimistic" literature with a special focus on the risks of social media for organizations and their reputation, in particular: user attacks on brands.

References

Alexandrov, A., Lilly, B., & Babakus, E. (2013). The effects of social- and self-motives on the intentions to share positive and negative word of mouth. *Journal of the Academy of Marketing Science*, 41(5), 531−546.

Asmussen, B., Harridge-March, S., Occhiocupo, N., & Farquhar, J. (2013). The multi-layered nature of the internet-based democratization of brand management. *Journal of Business Research*, 66(9), 1473−1483.

Avery, E. J., Lariscy, R. W., Kim, S., & Hocke, T. (2010). A quantitative review of crisis communication research in public relations from 1991 to 2009. *Public Relations Review*, 36(2), 190−192.

Brown, T. J., Barry, T. E., Dacin, P. A., & Gunst, R. F. (2005). Spreading the word: Investigating antecedents of consumers' positive word-of-mouth intentions and behaviors in a retailing context. *Journal of the Academy of Marketing Science*, 33(2), 123−138.

Coombs, W. T. (2004). Impact of past crises on current crisis communication: Insights from situational crisis communication theory. *Journal of Business Communication*, 41(3), 265−289.

Coombs, W. T. (2006). The protective powers of crisis response strategies. *Journal of Promotion Management*, 12(3−4), 241−260.

Coombs, W. T. (2007). Ongoing crisis communication. Planning, managing, and responding. Los Angeles, CA: Sage Publications.

Coombs, W. T., & Holladay, S. J. (1996). Communication and attributions in a crisis: An experimental study in crisis communication. *Journal of Public Relations Research*, 8(4), 279−295.

Coombs, W. T., & Holladay, S. J. (2014). How publics react to crisis communication efforts: Comparing crisis response reactions across sub-arenas. *Journal of Communication Management*, 18(1), 40−57.

Dholakia, U. M., & Durham, E. (2010). How effective is Facebook marketing? *Harvard Business Review*, 88(3), 26, Reprint F1003E.

Divol, R., Edelman, D., & Sarrazin, H. (2012). Demystifying social media. *McKinsey Quarterly*, 2(12), 66−77.

East, R., Hammond, K., & Lomax, W. (2008). Measuring the impact of positive and negative word of mouth on brand purchase probability. *International Journal of Research in Marketing, 25*(3), 215–224.

Felix, R., Rauschnabel, P. A., & Hinsch, C. (2017). Elements of strategic social media marketing: A holistic framework. *Journal of Business Research, 70*, 118–126.

Hansen, N., Kupfer, A. K., & Hennig-Thurau, T. (2018). Brand crises in the digital age: The short-and long-term effects of social media firestorms on consumers and brands. *International Journal of Research in Marketing, 35*, 557–574.

Hennig-Thurau, T., Hofacker, C. F., & Bloching, B. (2013). Marketing the pinball way: Understanding how social media change the generation of value for consumers and companies. *Journal of Interactive Marketing, 27*(4), 237–241.

Hennig-Thurau, T., Malthouse, E. C., Friege, C., Gensler, S., Lobschat, L., Rangaswamy, A., & Skiera, B. (2010). The impact of new media on customer relationships. *Journal of Service Research, 13*(3), 311–330.

Johnen, M., Jungblut, M., & Ziegele, M. (2018). The digital outcry: What incites participation behavior in an online firestorm? *New Media & Society, 20*(9), 3140–3160.

Kaplan, A. M., & Haenlein, M. (2010). Users of the world, unite! The challenges and opportunities of Social Media. *Business Horizons, 53*(1), 59–68.

Kim, A. J., & Ko, E. (2012). Do social media marketing activities enhance customer equity? An empirical study of luxury fashion brand. *Journal of Business Research, 65*(10), 1480–1486.

Kristal, S., Baumgarth, C., & Henseler, J. (2018). "Brand play" versus "Brand attack": The subversion of brand meaning in non-collaborative co-creation by professional artists and consumer activists. *Journal of Product & Brand Management, 27*(3), 334–347.

Labrecque, L., vor dem Esche, J., Mathwick, C., Novak, T., & Hofacker, C. (2013). Consumer power: Evolution in the digital age. *Journal of Interactive Marketing, 27*(4), 257–269.

Langfield, A. (2014). Hotel apologizes after 3,000 bad reviews. *CNBC*. <https://www.cnbc.com/2014/08/05/hotel-apologizes-after-3000-bad-reviews.html>   Retrieved 09.12.18.

Li, C., & Bernoff, J. (2011). *Groundswell: Winning in a world transformed by social technologies.* Harvard Business Press.

Liu, B. F., Austin, L., & Jin, Y. (2011). How publics respond to crisis communication strategies: The interplay of information form and source. *Public Relations Review, 37*(4), 345–353.

Rauschnabel, P. A., Kammerlander, N., & Ivens, B. S. (2016). Collaborative brand attacks in social media: exploring the antecedents, characteristics, and consequences of a new form of brand crises. *Journal of Marketing Theory and Practice, 24*(4), 381–410.

Relling, M., Schnittka, O., Sattler, H., & Johnen, M. (2016). Each can help or hurt: Negative and positive word of mouth in social network brand communities. *International Journal of Research in Marketing, 33*(1), 42–58.

Schwarz, A. (2012). Stakeholder attributions in crises: The effects of covariation information and attributional inferences on organizational reputation. *International Journal of Strategic Communication, 6*(2), 174–195.

Sivertzen, A., Nilsen, E., & Olafsen, A. (2013). Employer branding: Employer attractiveness and the use of social media. *Journal of Product & Brand Management, 22*(7), 473–483.

Zhang, J. Q., Craciun, G., & Shin, D. (2010). When does electronic word-of-mouth matter? A study of consumer product reviews. *Journal of Business Research, 63*(12), 1336–1341.

THE DARK SIDE OF SOCIAL MEDIA USE FOR SOCIETIES

CHAPTER

8

Social Media Privacy

WHAT IS PRIVACY?

Privacy can be defined as the control of who has access to information about the self. It serves multiple psychological functions, including (1) *personal autonomy*, in that we are free from manipulation by others and therefore control our own lives; (2) *emotional release* or "down time;" (3) *self-evaluation*, providing a space to process and evaluate our experience; and (4) *limited and protected communication*, which can help build trust and intimacy (Westin, 1967).

Livingstone (2008) argued that privacy is not being tied to disclosing certain types of information, but it is about control and who knows what about us. Different people might have a different definition of private information. That is why privacy cannot be entirely maintained by individuals. Marwick and Boyd (2014) suggested that when discussing privacy on social media, we need to study it as a "networked privacy." For example, our network—including our spouses, best friends, and parents—can publish information about us online that we did not approve. Disliking it can lead to privacy turbulence. Petronio (2002) discussed privacy turbulence and privacy ownership and boundaries, as a part of her communication privacy management (CPM) theory.

The first of the principles of the CPM theory is privacy ownership. We believe that our private information belongs to us. Following this is the second principle of privacy control—in that people feel they should have the right to control access to their personal information.

When access to private information is closed, boundaries are thick; when access is open, boundaries are thin. Building on this, the third principle is privacy rules, which help people decide whether to reveal personal information. The fourth principle is coownership. When information is shared, all involved are responsible to protect it. This may become a problem when using social media. Any information we post online makes other users and the social networking site coowners of the information—which could lead to privacy violations. Privacy turbulence is the fifth principle, in that trouble arises when unauthorized others gain access to personal information either accidentally or by someone's deliberate actions. CPM theory also highlights the importance of negotiating and enacting rules to manage personal information; if those rules are not followed, privacy turbulence occurs (Petronio, 2002). As Trepte (2015) argued, when facing social media privacy breaches, we need metacommunication—communication about communication. We ask ourselves how to handle private information online. Do we share pictures of our children? Not only do we have to negotiate these dilemmas with ourselves and other people, but we have to interact with the website provider as well. By adjusting our privacy settings or opting out of specific services, we are negotiating privacy with the website (Trepte, 2015).

CPM theory is helpful in accounting for the privacy paradox, since it can be argued that people find social media to be a convenient and efficient way to connect when a connection is desired—but also find it difficult to create boundaries when they are desired; this difficulty leads to privacy concerns. According to Boyd (2010b), "a conversation you might have in the hallway is private by default, public through effort," but on a Facebook wall "the conversation is public by default, private through effort." In other words, unlike face-to-face, information shared online is stored and archived and is easily replicated.

PRIVACY PARADOX AND SOCIAL MEDIA

Those who express concerns about online privacy do not always take proactive measures to protect that privacy. For example, we might complain about Facebook collecting and storing data about us, yet we continue posting on the site. Acquisti and Grossklags (2003) were among the first researchers to claim that the relationship between privacy attitudes and online disclosure of personal information was paradoxical. Three years later, Barnes (2006) coined the term "privacy paradox" to describe young people's behavior on social networking sites. In the past, teenagers would write journals that they kept private, but today those journals are posted online (in forms of tweets and Instagram photos) for others to read. Sharing this kind of information can put children in danger. Roesner, Gill, and Kohno (2014) found that 79.5% of Snapchat users know or suspect message recovery is possible, even though the premise of the app is that content disappears in 10 seconds or less; even so, over half of these users report they would not change their posting behavior if they found out that Snapchat was not secure.

So what is it about social media that makes it so attractive? Fox and Moreland (2015) proposed five affordances that are unique to social media. The first is *connectivity*, in that it allows users to connect with many other individuals at once. Second is *visibility*, in that information is more accessible than it would be offline and that messages between select people are also visible to third parties. Third is *social feedback*, in which users respond to and comment on each other's posts. Fourth is *persistence*, in that the content remains visible after the communication is finished and is difficult to remove. The fifth and final affordance is *accessibility*, in that users can communicate constantly throughout the day. These affordances create new communication patterns which can have negative consequences. This might include things such as finding a high school sweetheart and reconnecting through Facebook—or starting extramarital affairs on one of the dating websites where another person is available to "listen" to us 24/7.

Not everybody, however, is equally concerned with the privacy issue. Elueze and Quan-Haase (2018) placed adults into different privacy categories based on their online privacy attitudes. When it comes to privacy, people are either "fundamentalists," "pragmatists," or "marginally concerned." There are two subgroups of pragmatists: relaxed and intense. Privacy fundamentalists are suspicious about anything perceived to be a threat to their privacy and are unwilling to disclose personal information. They do not use social media, online banking, or e-commerce sites as they fear to be hacked or scammed online (Elueze & Quan-Haase, 2018). Pragmatists weigh the risks of giving out personal information with the potential rewards. Unconcerned individuals, on another hand, believe that their information is generally safe and are comfortable with sharing their information with organizations.

Elueze and Quan-Haase (2018) discovered that among participants 65–91 years old, most people were relaxed pragmatists (42% of the sample). They feel some desire to maintain their privacy online but, unlike intense pragmatists, they are less knowledgeable about the risks of sharing information online. The second largest category in the Elueze and Quan-Haase (2018) study was the marginally concerned group (25%). Marginally concerned individuals exhibit a low awareness of privacy risks online and feel that they are not at risk because their online activities are not relevant to their sensitive information.

Among college students, however, "Identity Loss" and "Future Life of Information" were the top privacy concerns (Quinn, 2016). Quinn (2016) did a survey study with 353 American undergraduate students to find out how privacy concerns and privacy behavior relate to the uses and gratifications of social media. When it comes to privacy behavior, users were concerned with professional use and reputation preservation. In addition, habit—as one of the gratifications students identified—was negatively associated with the use of privacy settings, blocking contacts, or restricting postviewability. These findings support previous research that found that lack of attention, lack of awareness, and lack of intentionality were indicators of habitual media use (LaRose, 2010).

In another study, Yang, Pulido, and Kang (2016) explored the relationship between privacy concerns and Twitter use among college students. They found that the control of privacy information on Twitter predicted college students' Twitter usage, as measured by minutes per day spent on Twitter; however, it did not predict the number of weekly logins. Their finding indicated that college students spent more time on Twitter when they perceived that they had control over their private information on the site.

There is also evidence that youths underestimate their frequency of posting with risky behaviors when asked to self-report, especially in light of their perceptions of how often their friends do so. For instance, Black, Schmiege, and Bull (2013) findings suggest that youth tend to overreport their friends' risky sexual behaviors, while underreporting the friends' protective sexual behaviors. The authors suggest this may be due to the "third-person effect," in which people believe others are much more susceptible to persuasive media than themselves (Davison, 1983). In addition, the third-person effect was used by Debatin, Lovejoy, Horn, and Hughes (2009) to interpret the finding that people think others' privacy is more so at risk than their own.

Consumer privacy. While membership on social media sites provides consumers with easy and convenient access to information that can help them make more informed purchases, it also puts their personal privacy at risk (Alba et al., 1997). Marketers have increasingly found value in advertising through social media and, in turn, the media have often highlighted consumer concerns over how their personal information is being used. For example, several studies have looked at the privacy paradox of consumers' social media engagement and online privacy protection behaviors. While consumers want to have control over how and with whom their information is shared, at the same time they are interested in building friendships online (Poddar, Mosteller, & Scholder-Ellen, 2009). This is another example of a privacy paradox.

Mosteller and Poddar (2017) drew on regulatory focus theory to propose that a person's behavior on social media sites is influenced by either a promotion or a prevention orientation to achieve a desired outcome. A consumer's behavior could be based on a promotion, in which case they will focus on potential gains from social media engagement. On the other hand a consumer with a prevention orientation would focus on avoiding negative outcomes from social media use; these negative outcomes could include the unwanted collection and sharing of their personal information (Poddar et al., 2009).

Most people, however, do not want their data to be shared with data collection companies without their knowledge. Yet, this is what social networking platforms have been doing for a decade now. Facebook has harvested user data for targeted advertising. The latest case includes Cambridge Analytica, which collected personally identifiable information of up to 87 million people. Privacy concerns are also the main reason for deactivating a Facebook account (Stieger, Burger, Bohn, & Voracek, 2013). Liu, Gummadi, Krishnamurthy, and Mislove (2011) measured Facebook users' disparity between the desired and actual privacy settings and found that Facebook privacy settings matched users' expectations only 37% of the time. It is therefore not surprising that more Americans trust the Internal Revenue Service than Facebook (Ekins, 2013).

Rauschnabel, He, and Ro (2018) did a study to examine if people really care about their own versus other people's privacy. They found that people generally tend to act as "satisficers," who tend to seek a satisfactory problem solution rather than an optimal one (Smith, Dinev, & Xu, 2011). They are also more sensitive to the risks whose consequences might occur sooner rather than later ("hyperbolic discounting," Smith et al., 2011). In other words, we care about short-term benefits more than long-term risks. So if a user can share his/her data and get compliments by followers, these benefits would result immediately. The risks, such as spam ads or not getting a job, may happen further away in the future.

Children's privacy. Parents have expressed concerns over their children's technology use, citing fears of "stranger danger," accessing adult content, and cyberbullying (Madden, Cortesi, Gasser, Lenhart, & Duggan, 2012). In turn, they have become more active in visiting their children's social media profiles, friending, and following their children on social media, and checking the websites that their children visit to keep up with their online activities (Anderson, 2016). However, teens sometimes combat this increased surveillance by using apps such as Snapchat or using social steganography (encapsulating a message so only the intended audience understands the true meaning) (Boyd, 2010a, 2014; Wisniewski, Xu, Rosson, Perkins, & Carroll, 2016).

CPM theory is relevant for examining how families negotiate technology use and privacy during late adolescence, since it provides a framework to evaluate the dialectical tensions in private disclosures (Petronio, 2002; Petronio & Durham, 2015). Differences in values regarding online privacy and teen technology use can lead to turbulence between parents and children. For instance, while teens often view online spaces as "private," parents generally view shared online content as "uncontrollable" and prefer to monitor or restrict it (Cranor, Durity, Marsh, & Ur, 2014). Online safety apps generally encourage parental control strategies, such as monitoring and restricting teens' online activities. Hawk, Hale, Raaijmakers, and Meeus (2008) found a connection between relationship satisfaction and boundary turbulence, such that teenagers that reported lower quality interactions with parents also perceived more boundary turbulence. It was also found that teens' perceptions of parental privacy invasions predicted parental conflict; teens who perceived more privacy invasions also reported more conflicts (Hawk, Keijsers, Hale, & Meeus, 2009).

Vitak, Liao, and Kumar (2018) also used CPT theory to explore factors leading to familial turbulence around technology use. They surveyed 96 parents and teen children. Parents were asked about their use of monitoring tools to track their child's online behaviors and their decision to connect with their child through social media platforms. Of all the parents who completed the survey, 27.2% reported installing monitoring apps or software to track their child's phone and Internet activities, and 88% of these parents said that their child was aware that they were being monitored. The parents who said that they were not currently monitoring their child but would consider it the future cited reasons of ensuring their child was acting appropriately and safely, and confirming that their child was following household rules about technology use. For parents who said they would not consider monitoring, they stated either that they trusted their child, their child was already open about technology use, or that they performed random checks of their child's devices. Almost half of the parent respondents (48%) reported they were friends with their child on at least one social media site; one main reason was to see what their child, or their child's friends, was posting online. Another reason was to share content such as links and images with their child. In many of the cases where parents were not friends with their child on any platforms, it was often because the parent was not on social media or the parent and child used different platforms.

Vitak et al. (2018) also asked about behaviors that were more likely to lead to turbulence. In their study, perceived parental restriction was positively related to privacy turbulence likelihood, meaning that teens who felt more restricted were also more likely to experience privacy turbulence due to misalignment and parental monitoring practices. In addition, privacy turbulence was more likely for older teens than younger ones. This might have been due to a greater desire for autonomy among older teens, which can lead to tension if they perceive a greater parental restriction.

Despite expressing privacy concerns, many parents still share information about their children, both online and on social media. However, children are not always in control of what their parents share about them. "Sharenting" is a term that has been used to describe the practice. While "sharenting" can have benefits such as raising money for research and advocacy or community support, the information that parents share about their children may hurt the children's life. Steinberg (2017) pointed out that "friends" on social media might use shared information about a child and potentially harm them. This is significant considering that 76% of kidnappings and 90% of violent crimes against children are committed by relatives and acquaintances. Steinberg (2017) proposed a set of the best practices focusing on children's well-being. Those include considering sometimes sharing anonymously, using caution before sharing their child's actual location, giving their child "veto power" over online disclosures, not sharing pictures in any state of undress, as well as considering the effects sharing can have on their child's current and future sense of self and well-being.

Kumar (2018) also argued that parental online sharing can be complicated, as such sharing can raise privacy concerns for the child. Kumar collected and analyzed a sample of posts from the blog "STFU, Parents," and described the three final norm statements that were identified by bloggers. The first advice was "No Gross Stuff," indicating that parents should not discuss or depict messy realities of human bodily functions. For example, the blog advocated against posts about toilet-related activities. The second norm statement was "Be Funny, Not Dramatic or Dull," indicating that parents should share content that is humorous, but they should not share content that is extremely emotional. For instance, some of the cases included rants at neighbors, delivery people, or workers who inconvenienced the parent in some way. The third norm was "Positive Presentation," in that parents should acknowledge the downsides of parenting but should not share content that portrays them in a negative light. Parents must take care not to overstate the risks of social media use to their children, for risk of losing credibility (Jordan et al., 2014; Lannin & Scott, 2013). Parents, but also other social media users, should be aware of privacy issues that are intertwined in online exposure.

However, most people will not protect their online lives appropriately because they lack online privacy literacy (Trepte et al., 2015).

PRIVACY LITERACY

Privacy literacy is defined as an "informed concern for users' privacy and effective strategies to protect it" (Debatin, 2011). Trepte et al. (2015) defined it as a combination of declarative (knowing that) and procedural (knowing how) knowledge about online privacy. Hong and Thong (2013) developed a scale to measure privacy concerns. The scale includes items such as, "It is very important to me that I am aware and knowledgeable about how my personal information will be used by commercial/government websites." Bartsch and Dienlin (2016) did a study with 630 Facebook users to uncover factors that potentially contribute to and result from online privacy literacy. Social privacy literacy measured the perceived skill to regulate privacy settings on Facebook. One example item was, "I know how to restrict access to profile information such as hobbies or interests." Bartsch and Dienlin (2016) found that users with high levels of privacy literacy also tended to have private profiles, and privacy literacy was associated with a higher perceived safety and actual privacy protective behaviors.

Wright and Bleakley (2018) also examined how privacy literacy and privacy perceptions on Facebook and Snapchat are associated with youths posting about alcohol, marijuana, and sexual activity online. However, their results were more nuanced in that a higher privacy literacy was associated with more frequent posts about alcohol on Snapchat. Although this finding was surprising, it may indicate that users feel more comfortable displaying such content on Snapchat due to its inherent privacy settings. In fact, the action of friends posting a respondent on their story smoking marijuana was positively associated with the respondent posting themselves smoking marijuana as well (Wright & Bleakley, 2018). The respondent receiving snaps that depicted drinking alcohol and sexual activity was positively associated with the respondent posting each behavior, respectively. On Facebook, however, respondents were more careful. Privacy literacy was associated with a decrease in respondents' overall risky behavior posting. Privacy perception was also negatively associated with posting about smoking marijuana (Wright & Bleakley, 2018). These results again indicate that people use different privacy settings depending on how safe they feel when using each networking site.

USES AND GRATIFICATIONS THEORY AND PRIVACY ON SOCIAL MEDIA

Privacy behavior is also related to social media gratifications. The uses and gratifications theory (Katz, 1959) posits that individuals have specific motives for using media, and they are active and goal-oriented in meeting their needs. Originally, these needs, or gratifications, were identified as *diversion* (escape from reality), *personal relationships* (using media for companionship), *personal identity* (reinforcing values), and *surveillance* (information that helps an individual accomplish something) (McQuail, Blumler, & Brown, 1972). For example, we use social media to stay in touch with family and friends who live in another city or another country. We watch online videos for entertainment, and we also turn on TV news channels that reflect and reinforce our political ideologies. In other words, the exact nature of gratifications derived through media use changes based on the specific medium (Sheldon, Rauschnabel, Antony, & Car, 2017). Social media behavior has also restructured the nature of gratifications. For example, while television generally fulfills information or entertainment needs, we tend to use social network sites to maintain and cultivate existing relationships (Sheldon, 2008). We use other social network sites such as LinkedIn to satisfy our professional advancement needs.

Most recently, research has focused on how social media use intersects with privacy activities; for instance, it has been found that many who use social media for entertainment are more likely to use anonymous profiles, while those who use it to communicate may focus on adjusting privacy settings (Lampe, Wash, Velasquez, & Ozkaya, 2010; Spiliotopoulos & Oakley, 2013). Spiliotopoulos and Oakley (2013) conducted a survey to examine the relationship between motives for Facebook use and their relationship to privacy attitudes. Results revealed that users go on Facebook for social connection, shared identity, photographs, content, social investigation, social network surfing, and newsfeed. When it comes to privacy, those who spent more time on Facebook were also more concerned about their privacy. Using Facebook for communicating with like-minded people or to organize events was also positively related to privacy concerns. Those individuals also reported changing their privacy settings more often.

CONCLUSION

Social media companies should take into account the privacy needs of the users; the practice of prioritizing the economic value of users over their right to privacy is concerning. Legislation on the federal level may be able to protect users' privacy beyond what technology companies' guidelines have, especially in instances of minor and employee privacy violations.

References

Acquisti, A., & Grossklags, J. (2003). *Losses, gains, and hyperbolic discounting: An experimental approach to information security attitudes and behavior.* Presented at the 2nd Annual Workshop on Economics and Information Security-WEIS 3, 1-27, Berkeley, CA.

Alba, J., Lynch, J., Weitz, B., Janiszewski, C., Lutz, R., Sawyer, A., & Wood, S. (1997). Interactive home shopping: Consumer, retailer, and manufacturer incentives to participate in electronic marketplaces. *Journal of Marketing, 61,* 38–53.

Anderson, M. (2016). *Parents, teens and digital monitoring.* Washington, DC: Pew Research Center: Internet, Science & Tech. Retrieved from http://www.pewinternet.org/2016/01/07/parents-teens-and-digital-monitoring/.

Barnes, S. (2006). A privacy paradox: Social networking in the United States. *First Monday, 11.* Available from https://doi.org/10.5210/fm.v11i9.1394.

Bartsch, M., & Dienlin, T. (2016). Control your Facebook: An analysis of online privacy literacy. *Computers in Human Behavior, 56,* 147–154. Available from https://doi.org/10.1016/j.chb.2015.11.022.

Black, S. R., Schmiege, S., & Bull, S. (2013). Actual versus perceived peer sexual risk behavior in online youth social networks. *Translational Behavioral Medicine, 3*(3), 312–319. Available from https://doi.org/10.1007/s13142-013-0227-y.

Boyd, D. (2010a). Social network sites as networked publics: Affordances, dynamics, and implications. In Z. Papacharissi (Ed.), *A networked self: Identity, community, and culture on social network sites* (pp. 39–58). Routledge.

Boyd, D. (2010b). Making sense of privacy and publicity. In: *SXSW.* Austin, TX.

Cranor, L. F., Durity, A. L., Marsh, A., & Ur, B. (2014). *Parents' and teens' perspectives on privacy in a technology-filled world. Proceedings of the Tenth Symposium on Usable Privacy and Security* (pp. 19–35). Menlo Park, CA: USENIX Association.

Davison, W. P. (1983). The third-person effect in communication. *Public Opinion Quarterly*, 47(1), 1–15. Available from https://doi.org/10.1086/268763.

Debatin, B. (2011). Ethics, privacy, and self-restraint in social networking. In S. Trepte, & L. Reinecke (Eds.), *Privacy online: Perspectives on privacy and self-disclosure in the social web* (pp. 47–60). Berlin, Heidelberg: Springer Berlin Heidelberg. https://doi.org/10.1007/978-3-642-21521-6_5.

Debatin, B., Lovejoy, J. P., Horn, A. K., & Hughes, B. N. (2009). Facebook and online privacy: Attitudes, behaviors, and unintended consequences. *Journal of Computer-Mediated Communication*, 15, 83–108. Available from https://doi.org/10.1111/j.1083-6101.2009.01494.x.

Ekins, E. (2013). *Poll: On privacy, IRS and NSA deemed more trustworthy than Facebook and Google*. Retrieved from <http://reason.com/poll/2013/09/27/poll-on-privacy-irs-and-nsa-deemed-more>.

Elueze, I., & Quan-Haase, A. (2018). Are older adults (65 +) privacy fundamentalists? Revisiting Westin's privacy attitude typology. In: *Paper presented to the International Communication Association conference*, Prague, Czech Republic.

Fox, J., & Moreland, J. J. (2015). The dark side of social networking sites: An exploration of the relational and psychological stressors associated with Facebook use and affordances. *Computers in Human Behavior*, 45, 168–176. Available from https://doi.org/10.1016/j.chb.2014.11.083.

Hawk, S. T., Hale, W. W., Raaijmakers, Q. A. W., & Meeus, W. (2008). Adolescents' perceptions of privacy invasion in reaction to parental solicitation and control. *The Journal of Early Adolescence*, 28, 583–608. Available from https://doi.org/10.1177/0272431608317611.

Hawk, S. T., Keijsers, L., Hale, W. W., & Meeus, W. (2009). Mind your own business! Longitudinal relations between perceived privacy invasion and adolescent-parent conflict. *Journal of Family Psychology*, 23(4), 511–520. Available from https://doi.org/10.1037/a0015426.

Hong, W., & Thong, J. Y. (2013). Internet privacy concerns: an integrated conceptualization and four empirical studies. *MIS Quarterly*, 37, 275–298. Retrieved from <http://papers.ssrn.com/sol3/papers.cfm?abstract_id = 2229627>.

Jordan, N. A., Russell, L., Afousi, E., Chemel, T., McVicker, M., Robertson, J., & Winek, J. (2014). The ethical use of social media in marriage and family therapy recommendations and future directions. *The Family Journal*, 22, 105–112. Available from https://doi.org/10.1177/1066480713505064.

Katz, E. (1959). Mass communications research and the study of popular culture: An editorial note on a possible future for this journal. *Studies in Public Communication*, 2, 1–6. Retrieved from <http://repository.upenn.edu/asc_papers/165>.

Kumar, P. (2018). Emerging norms and privacy implications of parental online sharing: The perspective of the STFU, Parents Blog. In: *Paper presented to the International Communication Association conference*, Prague, Czech Republic.

Lampe, C., Wash, R., Velasquez, A., & Ozkaya, E. (2010). Motivations to participate in online communities. In: *Proceedings of CHI '10* (p. 1927). New York: ACM. https://doi.org/10.1145/1753326.1753616.

Lannin, D. G., & Scott, N. A. (2013). Social networking ethics: Developing best practices for the new small world. *Professional Psychology, Research and Practice*, 44, 135–141. Available from https://doi.org/10.1037/a0031794.

LaRose, R. (2010). The problem of media habits. *Communication Theory*, 20, 194–222. Available from https://doi.org/10.1111/j.1468-2885.2010.01360.x.

Liu, Y., Gummadi, K., Krishnamurthy, B., & Mislove, A. (2011). Analyzing Facebook privacy settings: User expectations vs. reality. In: *Proceedings of the 2011 ACM SIGCOMM conference on Internet measurement conference* (pp. 61–70).

Livingstone, S. (2008). Taking risky opportunities in youthful content creation: Teenagers'
use of social networking sites for intimacy, privacy, and self-expression. New Media &
Society, 10, 339–411. Available from https://doi.org/10.1177/1461444808089415.

Madden, M., Cortesi, S., Gasser, U., Lenhart, A., & Duggan, M. (2012). Parents, teens, and
online privacy. Washington, DC: Pew Internet Project. Retrieved from <http://www.
pewinternet.org/2012/11/20/main-report-10/>.

Marwick, A. E., & Boyd, D. (2014). Networked privacy: How teenagers negotiate context
in social media. New Media & Society, 16(7), 1051–1067. Available from https://doi.
org/10.1177/1461444814543995.

McQuail, D., Blumler, J. G., & Brown, J. R. (1972). The television audience: Revised perspective. In D. McQuail (Ed.), Sociology of mass communications (pp. 135–165).
Harmondsworth: Penguin.

Mosteller., & Poddar. (2017). To share and protect: Using regulatory focus theory to examine the privacy paradox of consumers' social media engagement and online privacy
protection behaviors. Journal of Interactive Marketing, 39, 27–38.

Petronio, S. (2002). Boundaries of privacy: Dialectics of disclosure. Albany, NY: SUNY Press.

Petronio, S. (2013). Brief status report on communication privacy management theory.
Journal of Family Communication, 13, 6–14. Available from https://doi.org/10.1080/
15267431.2013.743426.

Petronio, S., & Durham, W. T. (2015). Communication privacy management theory:
Significance for interpersonal communication. In L. A. Baxter, & D. O. Braithwaite
(Eds.), Engaging theories in interpersonal communication: Multiple perspectives
(pp. 335–347). Sage.

Poddar, A., Mosteller, J., & Scholder-Ellen, P. (2009). Consumers' rules of engagement in
online information exchanges. Journal of Consumer Affairs, 43(3), 419–448.

Quinn, K. (2016). Why we share: A uses and gratifications approach to privacy regulation
in social media use. Journal of Broadcasting & Electronic Media, 60(1), 61–86.

Rauschnabel, P. A., He, J., & Ro, Y. K. (2018). Antecedents to the adoption of augmented
reality smart glasses: A closer look at privacy risks. Journal of Business Research, 92,
374–384.

Roesner, F., Gill, B. T., & Kohno, T. (2014). Sex, lies, or kittens? Investigating the use of
Snapchat's self-destructing messages. Lecture Notes in Computer Science (Including
Subseries Lecture Notes in Artificial Intelligence and Lecture Notes in Bioinformatics), 8437,
64–76. Available from https://doi.org/10.1007/978-3-662-45472-5_5.

Sheldon, P. (2008). The relationship between unwillingness to communicate and students'
Facebook use. Journal of Media Psychology: Theories, Methods, and Applications, 20, 67–75.
Available from https://doi.org/10.1027/1864-1105.20.2.6.

Sheldon, P., Rauschnabel, P., Antony, M. G., & Car, S. (2017). A cross-cultural comparison
of Croatian and American social network sites: Exploring cultural differences in
motives for Instagram use. Computers in Human Behavior, 75, 643–651. Available from
https://doi.org/10.1016/j.chb.2017.06.009.

Smith, H. J., Dinev, T., & Xu, J. (2011). Information privacy research: An interdisciplinary
review. MIS Quarterly, 35, 989–1016.

Spiliotopoulos, T., & Oakley, I. (2013). Understanding motivations for Facebook use. In:
Proceedings of CHI '13 (p. 3287). New York: ACM. https://doi.org/10.1145/
2470654.2466449.

Steinberg, S. B. (2017). Sharenting: Children's privacy in the age of social media. Emory
Law Journal, 66, 839–1007.

Stieger, S., Burger, C., Bohn, M., & Voracek, M. (2013). Who commits virtual identity suicide? Differences in privacy concerns, Internet addiction, and personality between
Facebook users and quitters. Cyberpsychology, Behavior, and Social Networking, 16,
629–634. Available from https://doi.org/10.1089/cyber.2012.0323.

Trepte, S. (2015). Social media, privacy, and self-disclosure: The turbulence caused by social media's affordances. *Social Media + Society, 1*(1). Available from https://doi.org/10.1177/2056305115578681.

Trepte, S., Teutsch, D., Masur, P. K., Eicher, C., Fischer, M., Hennhofer, A., et al. (2015). Do people know about privacy and data protection strategies? Towards the "online privacy literacy scale" (OPLIS). In S. Gutwirth, R. Leenes, & P. de Hert (Eds.), *Reforming European data protection law* (pp. 333–365). Heidelberg: Springer. Available from https://doi.org/10.1007/978-94-017-9385-8.

Vitak, J., Liao, Y., & Kumar, P. (2018). How communication technologies introduce privacy turbulence in families during late adolescence. In: *Paper presented at the International Communication Association conference.* Prague, Czech Republic.

Westin, A. F. (1967). *Privacy and freedom.* New York: Athenaeum.

Wisniewski, P., Xu, H., Rosson, M.B., Perkins, D.F., & Carroll, J.M. (2016). Dear diary: Teens reflect on their weekly online risk experiences. In: *Proceedings of the 2016 CHI conference on human factors in computing systems* (pp. 3919–3930). New York: ACM. https://doi.org/10.1145/2858036.2858317.

Wright, J. & Bleakley, A. (2018). Sex, drugs, and privacy settings: How privacy relates to youth risky behavior displays on social media. In: *Paper presented at the International Communication Association conference*, Prague, Czech Republic.

Yang, K. C., Pulido, A., & Kang, Y. (2016). Exploring the relationship between privacy concerns and social media use among college students: A communication privacy management perspective. *Intercultural Communication Studies, 25*(2), 46–62.

CHAPTER

9

Social Media Lies and Rumors

LYING AS A FORM OF DECEPTION

Most people have told a lie in their lifetime. In fact, an average person tells one to two lies per day (DePaulo, Kashy, Kirkendol, Wyer, & Epstein, 1996; Serota, Levine, & Boster, 2010). The reasons for individuals to tell lies can vary from staying out of trouble to trying to impress other people to trying to gain an advantage or benefit. According to Buller and Burgoon (1996), motivators for deception are instrumental or goal-oriented (e.g., to get a job), relational or social capital (e.g., preserving social media relationships), and identity (e.g., preserving one's reputation by deleting shameful photos from social media).

Lies are bad as they affect the distribution of power in society. They add to the power of the liar and reduce the power of those who have been deceived (Brennen, 2017). Most lies are told to people we know very well (Whitty, Buchanan, Joinson, & Meredith, 2012). Hancock, Thom-Santelli, and Ritchie (2004) found a significant difference for the rates of lying between face-to-face, telephone, instant message, and e-mail interactions; the highest rates occurred during phone conversations and the lowest rates with e-mail. Whitty et al.'s (2012) online diary study with United Kingdom college students revealed that individuals were more likely to lie on the telephone, followed by face-to-face. Although planned lies were rarer than spontaneous lies, they were perceived as more serious and were also more likely told via text messaging.

ONLINE DECEPTION AND DECEPTION USING SOCIAL MEDIA

Online deception is defined as a broad set of malicious practices that use the Internet as a medium to intentionally give a target an incorrect mental representation of the circumstances of a social exchange (Grazioli & Jarvenpaa, 2003). When making choices about what information to include, what to leave out, and whether to engage in deception, many people take advantage of the properties of computer-mediated communication (Toma, Hancock, & Ellison, 2008). One example is social media.

In most social media platforms, communication is asynchronous, giving deceivers an advantage for altering the content. Zahavi (1993) identified the difference between assessment signals that are difficult to fake (e.g., age in driver's license) and conventional signals that are easier to fake (e.g., dying your hair to appear younger). Social media do not require assessment signals and therefore provide an environment for easier deception. In fact, most people say that they have lied on social media simply because they know everyone else lies online (Drouin, Miller, Wehle, & Hernandez, 2016).

In social media, deception can involve content, sender, and communication channel all together (Tsikerdekis & Zeadally, 2014). Manipulating content is the common way to deceive others. For example, photos can be manipulated with a number of free airbrushing apps on the market. Sender deception is achieved by manipulating the sender's identity information. In fact, identity theft is a common example. Although they required greater technical skills, eavesdropping and modifying in-transit messages are examples of communication-channel deception (Tsikerdekis & Zeadally, 2014).

There are various techniques used to deceive others in social media environments, including bluffs, mimicry, fakery, white lies, evasions, exaggerations, and concealment (Tsikerdekis & Zeadally, 2014). In describing the different types of online deception, Drouin et al. (2016) found that online deception is more than just lying, and there are many ways to be dishonest on social media and the Internet. An individual does not have to post a blatant lie on their social media accounts to be dishonest and deceitful. In fact, in Drouin et al.'s (2016) study, most participants admitted that they were dishonest on internet sites, but that they were also under the impression other people were more dishonest on the sites than they were.

In Drouin et al.'s (2016) study, most subjects felt that physical appearances were most often lied about—and that people who lied did so to appear more attractive, adventurous, or just overall better online than they appeared offline. They believed that other people were lying about their appearances, so they felt comfortable lying about their own. If some people are using their social media posts to make them look better, then it should be acceptable for everyone else to do the same. When it came to different online venues, study participants expected others to be more honest on social media than on any of the other sites—which included anonymous chat rooms, online dating sites, and sexual communication websites. Even though people expected more honesty from social media sites, they still expected a level of dishonesty. Also, they used this expectation of lies and dishonest posts as a reason to justify their own to deceit (Drouin et al., 2016).

Whitty (2002) examined whether Australian college students are open and honest about themselves in chat rooms. The study revealed that people who spend the least amount of time in chat rooms per week were more likely to tell lies. Men lied more than women about their gender, occupation, education, and income. They tried to make them sound better than they actually were. These findings reflect traditional theories of romantic relationships. Women prefer men who are more intelligent, ambitious, and have higher socioeconomic status (Wright, 1999). Women, however, lied more for safety reasons. Younger people also lied more than older people for safety reasons. Younger women also withheld information so that others could not discover their identity (Whitty, 2002).

Donath (1998) outlines four types of online deception: trolling, category deception, impersonation, and identity concealment. Trolling is purposefully posting something online to provoke anger from other users. Category deception is lying about the social role you actually play in the society which includes your age or gender. Impersonation is pretending to be an entirely different person and can include the subcategories of catfishing and scamming. Identity concealment is purposefully hiding part of, or the whole of, your identity so other individuals do not know who you are (Donath, 1998; Drouin et al., 2016). Research has shown that category deceptions are reported much more commonly than outright impersonations.

CATFISHING

Catfishing is one form of impersonation. It is defined by most people as a phenomenon of Internet scammers who fabricate online identities and entire social circles to trick people into romantic relationships (Peterson, 2013). A deceiver creates a fake profile on a social network site with the motive to trick people into thinking that they are someone else. They can use fake photos, fake biographies, and fake social network. Though online deception has always been a part of social media, only recently has the topic of "catfishing" been so prominent in the media. The term was made popular after a documentary film (2010) by the same name. Catfishing is a good reminder that we see what others want us to see when it comes to crafting an identity. Most people edit their real selves in face-to-face lives as well, showing the ideal and presented self instead. For example, for a Facebook profile photo, most people will pick the one where they thought they looked good. Social media are not instantaneous and, therefore, there is more time to edit the profile that others see. Adolescents and young adults often experiment with their online identities, pretending to be someone else (Manago, Graham, Greenfield, & Salimkhan, 2008).

SELF-PRESENTATION LIES

In his book *The Presentation of Self in Everyday Life*, Goffman (1959) described social life by using theatrical metaphors. According to the metaphors, we are all performers who take on unique roles in different situations. He distinguished between the signals that we "give" intentionally and those we "give off" unintentionally. Intentional signals are used to convey a particular impression to others. Computer-mediated communication allows us to present ourselves more selectively than is possible face-to-face. Internet has been described as a playground where people can try on different personalities (Rheingold, 1993).

In an online dating context, for example, users try to present themselves as attractive as possible. In a Hancock, Toma, and Ellison's (2007) study, 81% of online dating users lied about their age, weight, or height. Ellison, Heino, and Gibbs (2006) argued that such deceptions are not always intentional, as users might subconsciously describe their "ideal self." According to Walther's theory of hyperpersonal interaction, asynchronous messages and reduced communication cues contribute to selective self-presentation in computer-mediated settings. Not only do users have more time for message construction, but they also have more control over what cues are sent (Walther, 2007).

Vishwanath (2014) conducted an experiment to discover if the factor of habitual Facebook uses impacted an individual's likelihood to be deceived on social media. To test this, 150 senior undergraduate students from the University of Buffalo were studied. At the beginning of the semester, the students were given a survey that asked the students about their technology use. The survey included questions about their Facebook use: how often or habitually had they used it, the size of their social network on Facebook, if they had any concerns about privacy, their attitudinal commitment, and if they were able to self-regulate time spent on Facebook. Six weeks after the pertinent background survey was completed, a fake Facebook account for a fictitious person was created and friend requests from this fake account were sent to each of the student participants. The experimenters wanted to see which of the students fell for the deceit and accepted the false friend request (Vishwanath, 2014). Though in this case the fake account was controlled by the experimenters who had no malicious intent, other fake Facebook accounts exist and are used by Phishers, catfishers, and scammers, and can be dangerous when people allow fake account holders to follow their social media accounts. In this study the student participants were unaware that the fake account had been created merely to complete the study and that there would be no consequences to accepting the request. This is why the act of sending friend requests from this fake profile is perceived as deceptive, and, if the sender intended ill will, could be seen as a social media attack.

The experiment continued with yet another phase. An e-mail designed to look like a Phishing attempt was sent to the participants. The e-mail claimed that the students were eligible for an internship opportunity, and all the students had to do was respond with their full name, student identification number, and full birthdate. The e-mail included purposeful grammatical errors and a time limit which the e-mail recipient had to respond, by to make it look like common Phishing attempts. The purpose was to see which of the students would respond to the e-mail and divulge the personal information that was requested of them. The experimenters concluded from their study that those who fell for the deception and were more often victims of social media attacks were habitual Facebook users. Vishwanath (2014) defined being a habitual Facebook user as someone who uses Facebook frequently, has a large social network of people on Facebook, and is not good at or is unable to regulate their social media behaviors.

III. THE DARK SIDE OF SOCIAL MEDIA USE FOR SOCIETIES

He explains why these young, highly educated students fell for the social media attacks. "...Once a media behavior becomes habitual, it usually leads to patterned actions that are enacted whenever the situation or urge presents itself, without further reflection on the merits of the behavior" (Vishwanath, 2014, p. 87). It appears that the more one uses social media, the more of a habit it becomes, and the less one thinks about the decisions that come with participating actively on social media. If a fake friend request is sent to a user's account, a habitual Facebook user may accept their request without a second thought. With one click, he can grant a stranger total access to his Facebook page and all his and his friends' information, with no regard for the requestors intent on how they will use this information.

MISINFORMATION AND RUMORS

Social media are able to proliferate rumors more rapidly and broadly than traditional media (Castillo, Mendoza, & Poblete, 2013). Social ties are regarded as an important, influential factor in the formation of rumors, since people tend to believe those they feel close to (Garrett, 2011). Oh, Agrawal, and Rao (2013) studied conditions under which rumors spread on Twitter. They revealed that information with no clear source provided, personal involvement, and anxiety during crises were the most significant causes of rumors on social media. With the absence of gatekeepers, citizen journalists can publish erroneous information that is spread to a global audience in seconds. A recent example includes the April 2013 Boston bombings. After the bombings, social media users engaged in an attempt to identify the bombers from photos of the scene and incorrectly speculated that a missing student was one of the bombers. Misinformation on social media still represents a challenge for those seeking to use social media during crises (Starbird, Maddock, Orand, Achterman, & Mason, 2014). Media can also exacerbate audience fears through "mean world syndrome." Gerbner and Gross (1976) proposed cultivation theory to explain how television news concerning violence can convince viewers that the outside world is more dangerous than it actually is. The recent example is anti-Muslim rhetoric.

Another large part of social media deception is the spreading of rumors. Zubiaga, Liakata, Procter, Hoi, and Tolmie (2016) defined a rumor as a "circulating story of questionable veracity, which is apparently credible but hard to verify, and produces sufficient skepticism and/or anxiety so as to motivate finding out the actual truth" (p. 2). The authors analyzed cases of breaking news they believed would provoke the spread of rumors and specific rumors that Twitter users were posting about. Cases of breaking news studied included the Ferguson unrest, Ottawa shooting, Sydney siege, Charlie Hebdo shooting, and Germanwings plane crash. The specific rumors studied were that Prince was going to have a secret concert in Toronto, that the Bern Museum of Fine Arts was going to accept and display an art collection from a Nazi-era art dealer's son, that Russian president Vladimir Putin was sick or dead after not appearing in public for several days, and that athlete Michael Essien had contracted the Ebola virus. The authors tracked hashtags and keywords related to the events and chose to observe rumor candidates who had large numbers of retweets. The study found that rumors that could quickly be proven true or false didn't spark much attention, but rumors that remained unverified as to whether they were true or false were the ones that received the most attention and were retweeted the most. "This analysis reveals an interesting pattern in behavior, showing that users tend to support unverified rumors (whether explicitly or implicitly), potentially due to the arousal that these early, unverified stories produce and their potential societal impact" (Zubiaga et al., 2016, p. 17). They also found that true rumors are resolved more quickly than their false counterparts (Zubiaga et al., 2016). This makes sense because if a rumor is true, there will likely be evidence to prove it is, in fact, true, but if a rumor is false, there are probably few ways to prove it wrong. Also, if a rumor has already been proven true or false, there's no fun in the mystery of the rumor and guessing what the truth may be. Unverified rumors are more interesting because you don't actually know if they're true or not and you can wonder and guess about it. People can also retweet these unverified rumors asking if others have heard the news and can create a discussion and interaction in their online community of Twitter followers and possible gain new followers. In Zubiaga et al.'s study, once the rumors were proven either right or wrong, no one cared about them or retweeted them anymore, but the unverified rumors continued to be shared and spread across Twitter.

One of the great benefits of social media is that people are able to stay connected all the time, even in times of crisis. However, in the face of crises, rumors often tend to surface and spread like wildfire. With large amounts of information circulating throughout social media during a time of crisis, it can be difficult to determine what is accurate, how serious the situation actually is, and what precautions or preventions need to be taken. This can cause a lot of anxiety and stress for people, which is why it is important for those with information to step forward and dispel any false information and rumors that are spreading about the situation.

Zhao, Yin, and Song (2016) discussed how rumors are spread on social media during disasters and crises and how people choose to combat those rumors. The study was conducted through an online survey distributed to 400 participants throughout China. The authors used the Theory of Planned Behavior (TPB) and the Norm Activated Model (NAM). The TPB explains the motives and influences behind a person's particular behavior. The NAM is used to understand what is expected by society and what is prosocial behavior. The authors used the TPB as a basis for their study using the variables that the original theory uses to explain behavior: "attitude toward the behavior, subjective norm, perceived behavioral control and behavioral intention" (Zhao et al., 2016, p. 3).

The results from Zhao et al.'s(2016) study revealed that more and more people are becoming aware of the consequences of spreading rumors. They found that during a crisis, social media users are likely to dispel rumors they see if they have the knowledge and resources to do so (Zhao et al., 2016). The study was able to support multiple hypotheses including that "attitudes toward the rumor combating behavior will positively influence social media users' intention to combat rumors in times of social crisis"—and "Subjective norms will positively influence social media users' intention to combat rumors in a time of social crisis" (Zhao et al., 2016, p. 3). Citizen's overall attitudes that they should and are expected to call out false rumors drive them to share information regarding rumors that they see appear. The study also suggests that emergency workers and first responders receive a social media training to help stop the spread of rumors. A lack of information in a crisis will often lead to rumors being posted and shared, and information that is posted without a source can heighten anxiety in a crisis situation. If first responders are posting information about a crisis to an official account, people will know they can trust the information they are receiving. If rumors start to spread during the crisis, the first responders will be able to quickly squash the false information and bring ease and accurate information to people who may have been misled by the rumors (Zhao et al., 2016).

FAKE NEWS

Fake news is "made-up news," manipulated to look like credible journalistic reports but are designed to deceive us (Brennen, 2017). Fake news has existed for a long time. The origins date back to preprinting era. Burkhardt (2017) showed evidence that fake news has been around as long as humans have lived in groups where power matters. During preprinting press era, only the leaders of the group (emperors, religious, and military leaders) had control of knowledge and information.

People have been spreading fake news for centuries in order to discredit political opponents and even propel countries into war. Sixth-century historian Procopius of Caesarea released a treaty called *Secret History* that discredits the Emperor Justinian. With the invention of the printing press and the spread of literacy, it became harder to mislead people (Burkhardt, 2017). However, different pamphlets and scandal sheets (called "libelles") were still created in the 18th century France. A French variation of fake news was known as the canard. Canard stands for an unfounded rumor or story. Canards were popular during the 17th century in France (Burkhardt, 2017).

In 1835, in the United States, the New York Sun published *The Great Moon Hoax*, falsely citing astronomer John Herschel as claiming to have discovered life on the moon. Written by a reporter named Richard Adams Locke, the articles were very convincing to the public that purchased them (Pressman, 2012). The New York Sun was one of many new "penny press" papers that sold many papers fast and cheap. The sales of the paper skyrocketed as the paper printed stories that detailed life on the moon including sightings of unicorns, bat-people, vegetation, and other life forms (Zielinski, 2015). Locke later said that the stories were meant as a satire reflecting on the influence that religion had on science. But readers were convinced of its authenticity partly because the findings were attributed to the Edinburg Journal of Science, which was a real entity that had stopped publication several years before. The stories even reached international attention with reprintings appearing in papers across Europe. An Italian publication even included beautiful lithographs detailing what Herschel had discovered (Zielinski, 2015). Ultimately, it was later revealed that the stories were a hoax. The public generally felt amused about the hoax experience.

In 1844 American writer Edgar Allan Poe wrote a hoax newspaper article claiming that a balloonist had crossed the Atlantic in a hot-air balloon in only 3 days (Burkhardt, 2017). Poe is credited with writing at least six stories that were fake news (Arevalo, 2017). His first hoax, Unparalled Adventures of Hans Pfall, was published in the *Southern Literary Messenger* in June 1835 (Boese, 2015). The account detailed a man who'd traveled to and settled on the moon. As the story went, he sent a note with a moon inhabitant to be delivered to earth. The second hoax, The Narrative of Arthur Gordon Pym, was published in the *Southern Literary Messenger* in January and February of 1837. This time, the story centered around a polar exploration that was a mystery to Americans at the time. Poe's third hoax, The Journal of Julius Rodman, appeared in *Burton's Gentlemen's Magazine* between January and June 1840. The story detailed a 1792 expedition led by Julius Rodman up the Missouri River, which would make Rodman the first European to cross the Rocky Mountains (Boese, 2015). The story was so convincing that the US Senate corroborated the story based on fictitious journals written by Poe. His fourth hoax, The Great Balloon Hoax, was published in the *New York Sun* in April 1844. The story detailed the first hot-air balloon named the Victoria traveling across the Atlantic. People were so excited, and the hoax was viewed as major news. It was quickly identified as a hoax as Poe himself, revealed the fact. The fifth hoax, Facts in the Case of M. Valdemar, appeared in the *American Whig Review's* December issue. The story centered around hypnosis and its ability to suspend death. The story gained publicity in America as well as Europe. An American hypnotist even corroborated the story as he claimed to have accomplished the same feat (Boese, 2015). The final hoax, Von Kempelen's Discovery, was published in *The Flag of Our Union's* April 1849 edition. It described the discovery by a German chemist, Baron Von Kempelen, of an alchemical process to transform lead into gold (Boese, 2015).

In the early 20th century and the beginning of the Cold War, most American newspapers reported fake news on Russia (Herman, 2017). Walter Lippmann, an American journalist, and Charles Merz, editorial page editor of the *New York Times*, did a study in 1920 to examine press coverage of the Russian Bolshevik revolution (1917–20). They found that the *New York Times'* news stories were not based on facts, but often reported on the events that did not happen. According to Lippmann and Merz (1920), strong editorial bias fed into news reporting. Even after 1920, the fake news did not stop.

One of the 20th-century examples of fake news is the Orson Welles's *War of the Worlds* broadcast in 1938. Welles who worked for CBS radio aired a dramatic production of H.G. Wells' War of the Worlds with his Mercury Theater on Air company. On live radio, scenes played out of a Martian invasion in New Jersey. For weeks, Welles and his colleagues had worked frantically to perfect the drama as it was set to air the night prior to Halloween. The over-the-top theatrics and dramatization of such a bizarre circumstance were thought to ensure that audiences would not only enjoy the program but appreciate its artistry. That could not have been further from the truth. Hysteria ensued. Audiences mistook fiction for fact and not only believed that the invasion took place but feared the aftermath. Listeners panicked and called police, newspapers, and radio stations for answers. The morning after, newspapers ran headlines reporting about mass stampedes, suicides, and listeners threatening to shoot Welles on sight (Schwartz, 2015). Scared of losing both his livelihood and life, Welles was forced to hold a press conference to explain his intentions. He and his colleagues alike asserted that they never thought anyone would assume that such a far-fetched story would be mistaken for anything other than entertainment (Schwartz, 2015). Since then, Welles' adaptation of *War of the Worlds* has been classified as one of the most controversial moments in broadcasting history (Memmott, 2013).

Fake news abounded in press coverage during the Vietnam War as well. The Vietnam War was a long and controversial war. It was a fight between North and South Vietnam that garnered military support from major powers in the world, most notably the United States and the Soviet Union. Communist North Vietnam got its support from the Soviet Union while South Vietnam received its assistance from the United States. Lasting effects of the war continued the Cold War between opposing military powers of the United States and the Soviet Union (Spector, 2018). In America, the war was viewed, unlike any other war before it. The culmination of long-standing confusion as to the purpose of the war and the social climate of peace and love in the late 1960s and 1970s made public support of the war minimal. Protestors openly opposed American administration and criticized both the war and the soldiers fighting in it. For the first time in the history of America, soldiers came home to a public that did not honor them. They were met at airports with protests and signs condemning them. Vietnam is often referred to as the "first television war" (Curley, 2016). The media's in the war has been classified as a controversy. It is believed that the media played a big role in the loss of the war by negative reporting—which helped to undermine support for the war in America. The media's nonstop and uncensored coverage also provided valuable information to the enemy in Vietnam (Curley, 2016). There're also the lingering questions of whether the "fake news" was that of the journalists or the government itself. Government officials had also been questioned about its positivist spin on the news coming from Vietnam. In fact, many of the journalists who were reporting were stationed in Saigon and obtained their information from briefings that would take place at the Saigon Hotel. These "five o'clock follies" or briefing sessions were orchestrated by government officials (Homonoff, 2017). For example, official government reports passed on to media characterized the opposing army as weak, outnumbered, and of minimal threat. When the Battle of Hue commenced on January 31, 1968, reports from journalists who were there on the American base, shocked the nation. Hue was being taken over by a substantial army that was a very real and legitimate threat. Government official vehemently denied the size and effectiveness of the opposition, but the reports of many journalists including Gene Roberts and Walter Cronkite, provided contradictory stories (Bowden, 2017). Ultimately, the truth about the war and casualties suffered helped to justify an already opposing American public.

Fake News on Social Media. Social media have contributed to a widespread distribution of fake news, as individual users, also known as "citizen journalists," can reach as many readers as traditional media used to. In 2016 62% of US adults got news from social media (Gottfried & Shearer, 2016). With the overwhelming amount of information, it is impossible for anyone to know something about everything. Since people cannot know everything, they are vulnerable to being misinformed and must try to determine which source is trusted (Burkhardt, 2017). This is especially troubling considering that many of the uploaded videos and photos of social media are edited to fit a chosen narrative (Crate, 2017). In addition, social media are also funded by advertisers more than they were in the past. Advertisers indirectly influence what is published on a website. Because most people are attracted to rumors, gossip, and scandals, there is an increased economic incentive to supply the public with fake news (Burkhardt, 2017). In other words, creating fake news website draws traffic to the website which is highly profitable (Holan, 2016).

During the 2016 US presidential election campaign, multiple fake news reports went viral on Facebook and Twitter. Many people who saw fake news stories reported that they believed them (Silverman & Singer-Vine, 2016). Guess, Nyhan, and Reifler (2018) found that approximately one in four Americans visited a fake news website from October 7 to November 14, 2016. They also found that Facebook was a medium where most of them were exposed to fake news. Fact-checks of fake news almost never happened.

The most discussed fake news stories favored Donald Trump over Hillary Clinton (Silverman, 2016). One example of a fake news story included a report about Pope Francis endorsing Donald Trump's presidential candidacy. The story was published on wtoe5news.com. Although wtoe5news.com is a satire and fantasy news website, this disclaimer was not included in the article, and the story was shared more than one million times on Facebook (Allcott & Gentzkow, 2017).

Fake news website often resembles those of legitimate news organizations (e.g., WashingtonPost.com.co, USAToday.com.co, NationalReport. net). However, they are often short-lived (Allcott & Gentzkow, 2017). Some of the reasons for providing fake news include drawing advertising revenues. For example, despite being opposed to Trump, Paul Horner produced pro-Trump stories for profit. Other reasons include advancing candidates they favor.

PAUL HORNER SUMMARY

Paul Horner was an American writer who served as the lead writer for National Report, a "fake news" website, from 2013 to 2014. Upon his departure from National Report, he created his own website News

continued

(cont'd)

Examiner in which he continued to produce fake news stories shared through the internet. Horner is most notably known for his contribution to the "fake news" hysteria during the 2016 Presidential Election. According to CBS news, Horner's stories had a great impact on public opinion during the campaign due to his fake news stories showing up on reputable sites such as Google, ABC News, and Fox News. For example, in 2016 Horner produced a story with the headline reading, "The Amish in America Commit Their Vote to Donald Trump; Mathematically Guaranteeing Him a Presidential Victory" (Daro, 2016). The story was published to abcnews.com.co, a website created by Horner. Association with the reputable name (ABC) led both readers and industry professionals to believe the authenticity of the story. The story was even classified as a legitimate article under the ABC search engine with Google (Daro, 2016). In an interview with CNN's Anderson Cooper, Horner stated that his stories were strictly satirical. He further went on to explain his method of creating a realistic or believable "fake news" story. "[...] the headline might be fake, the first paragraph might be fake, and then the rest of the story it's a lot of it's mostly political satire" (CNN, 2016). When charged with spreading false information, Horner responded by saying, "I do it to try and educate people. I see certain things wrong in society that I don't like how are [being] educated" (CNN, 2016). Horner was successful in his misinformation of the public for several reasons. Much of his news was linked to a political scandal that appealed to specific audiences. For example, Fox News covered a story written by Horner claiming that Barack Obama had funded a Muslim museum during the government shutdown of 2013 (Wemple, 2013). Horner most often connected many of his websites to names that were reputable such as ABC, CNN, CBS, and NBC. Horner was subsequently found deceased in his home. His death was ruled an accidental overdose. Horner was 38 years old (Caron, 2017).

Fake News Detection. Bond and DePaulo (2006) analyzed the results of more than 200 lie detection experiments and found that humans can detect lies in text only slightly better than by random chance. Computer experts, however, have tried to implement multiple approaches to the automatic recognition of false information (Burkhardt, 2017). One of those approaches is linguistic. Linguistic approach looks at the word patterns and word choices (Hancock, Woodworth, & Porter, 2013).

Certain patterns can reliably indicate that information is untrue. For example, deceptive writers tend to use verbs and personal pronouns more often, while truthful writers tend to use more nouns, adjectives, and propositions (Hardalov, Koychev, & Nakov, 2016). Another approach is to compare the written text from a number of authors. The comparison can show anomalies (Rubin & Lukoianova, 2015). The social media platforms themselves have made some effort to detect and flag fake news. Facebook has turned over the verification of information to third-party fact-checking organizations, including factcheck.org and snopes.com (Bell, 2016).

Media literacy to detect fake news. Crate (2017) offered a set of advices for educators who have a responsibility to teach students to be active citizens. Crate (2017) advises to examine the online news sources, see who authored the article, as well as who sponsors the page. In many cases, sponsors or advertisers have a control over what information is presented. Next advice includes checking for source reliability, or where the information in the article is coming from. Media literacy classes could help students have a better understanding of what real news is. One of the reasons that fake news spreads is because people click "share" without reading beyond the headline or thinking about the content of the article (Burkhardt, 2017). Before sharing the story, one should verify with a fact-checking site (such as snopes.com, politifact.com, stopfake.org, or factcheck.org) first to see what it has to say about the story.

CONCLUSION

In conclusion, social media can be a wonderful resource to a lot of people- it can keep people connected to others and keep people informed, however it can also be a medium for lies, deceit, and rumors. Due to social media's design, anyone can create a social media account and post anything they wish to on it, which can lead to dishonesty.

When it comes to social media deception it's not just black and white lies or truth, but many forms and shades of gray. Tsikerdekis and Zeadally (2014) explain that social media deception is more difficult to study than face-to-face communication. While there are many existing communication theories and research methods, they rely heavily on verbal and nonverbal cues that are not always available on online forums, so the interactions online are not always able to be studied the same way. Though social media has given us a new medium through which we can lie more easily, it has also created a medium that is more difficult for communications professionals to study those deceptions. Tsikerdekis and Zeadally (2014) are calling upon social media developers to jump into action to help prevent online deception. They propose that social media sites need to have some form of identity verification when accounts are created to prevent others from being deceived by phony accounts. It is important to understand that communication and interactions on social media are still interactions. Individuals are capable of lying and deceiving online just as easily as they're able to in face-to-face interactions, but they're able to hide it more easily.

References

Allcott, H., & Gentzkow, M. (2017). Social media and fake news in the 2016 election. *Journal of Economic Perspectives*, *31*(2), 211–236. Available from https://doi.org/10.1257/jep.31.2.211.

Arevalo, G. (2017).*The six hoaxes of Edgar Allan Poe*. Retrieved February 13, 2018, from <https://hubpages.com/literature/The-Six-Hoaxes-of-Edgar-Allan-Poe>.

Bell, E. (2016). *Facebook drains the fake news swamp with new, experimental partnerships. Little green footballs.* Retrieved from <http://littlegreenfootballs.com/page/322423_Facebook_Drains_the_Fake_News_>.

Boese, A. (2015). *Hoaxes of Edgar Allan Poe*. Retrieved February 13, 2018, from <http://hoaxes.org/archive/permalink/edgar_allan_poe>.

Bond, C. F., & DePaulo, B. M. (2006). Accuracy of deception judgments. *Personality and Social Psychology Review*, *10*, 214–234.

Bowden, M. C. (2017). *'Fake News' is a tactic of the Vietnam War*. Retrieved February 5, 2018from <http://time.com/4839971/trump-media-press-enemy-vietnam-war/>.

Brennen, B. (2017). Making sense of lies, deceptive propaganda, and fake news. *Journal of Media Ethics*, *32*, 179–181. Available from https://doi.org/10.1080/23736992.2017.1331023.

Buller, D. B., & Burgoon, J. K. (1996). Interpersonal deception theory. *Communication Theory*, *3*, 203–242.

Burkhardt, J. M. (2017). Combating fake news in the digital age. *Library Technology Reports*, *53*(8), 5.

Caron, C. (2017). *Paul Horner, fake news writer who took credit for Trump victory, dies at 38.* Retrieved February 05, 2018, from <https://www.nytimes.com/2017/09/27/business/media/paul-horner-dead-fake-news.html>.

Castillo, C., Mendoza, M., & Poblete, B. (2013). Predicting information credibility in time-sensitive social media. *Internet Research*, *23*(5), 560–588. Available from https://doi.org/10.1108/INTR-05-2012-0095.

CNN. (2016). *Fake news writer: I'm trying to educate people.* Retrieved February 05, 2018, from <https://www.youtube.com/watch?v = VSkgPr31Bgs&feature = youtu.be>.

Crate, L. (2017). Fake news vs. real news. *Education Digest*, *83*(1), 4.

Curley, R. (2016). *The Vietnam War and the media*. Retrieved February 5, 2018, from <https://www.britannica.com/topic/The-Vietnam-War-and-the-media-2051426>.

Daro, I. N. (2016). *How a prankster convinced people the Amish would win Trump the election.* Retrieved February 05, 2018, from <https://www.buzzfeed.com/ishmaeldaro/paul-horner-amish-trump-vote-hoax?utm_term = .gsgmq6rLz#.levzvdNG4>.

DePaulo, B. M., Kashy, D. A., Kirkendol, S. E., Wyer, M. M., & Epstein, J. A. (1996). Lying in everyday life. *Journal of Personality and Social Psychology*, *70*, 979–995.

Donath, J. S. (1998). Identity and deception in the virtual community. In M. A. Smith, & P. Kollock (Eds.), *Communities in cyberspace* (pp. 29–59). New York: Routledge.

Drouin, M., Miller, D., Wehle, S. M., & Hernandez, E. (2016). Why do people lie online? "Because everyone lies on the internet". *Computers in Human Behavior, 64*, 134–142.

Ellison, N., Heino, R., & Gibbs, J. (2006). Managing impressions online: Self-presentation processes in the online dating environment. *Journal of Computer-Mediated Communication, 11*(2), 415–441. Available from https://doi.org/10.1111/j.1083-6101.2006.00020.x.

Garrett, R. K. (2011). Troubling consequences of online political rumoring. *Human Communication Research, 37*(2), 255–274.

Gerbner, G., & Gross, L. (1976). Living with television: The violence profile. *Journal of Communication, 26*, 172–199.

Goffman, E. (1959). *The presentation of self in everyday life*. New York: Anchor Books.

Gottfried, J., & Shearer, E. (2016). *News use across social media platforms 2016*. Pew Research Center. Retrieved from <http://www.journalism.org/2016/05/26/news-use-acrosssocial-media-platforms-2016>.

Grazioli, S., & Jarvenpaa, S. L. (2003). Deceived: Under target online. *Communications of the ACM, 46*, 196–205.

Guess, A., Nyhan, B., & Reifler, J. (2018). *Selective exposure to misinformation: Evidence from the consumption of fake news during the 2016 U.S. presidential campaign*. Retrieved from <https://www.dartmouth.edu/~nyhan/fake-news-2016.pdf>.

Hancock, J. T., Thom-Santelli, J., & Ritchie, T. (2004). Deception and design: The impact of communication technology on lying behavior. *CHI Letters, 6*(1), 129–134.

Hancock, J. T., Toma, C., & Ellison, N. (2007). The truth about lying in online dating profiles. In: *Proceedings of the SIGCHI conference on human factors in computing systems pages*.

Hancock, J. T., Woodworth, M. T., & Porter, S. (2013). Hungry like the wolf: A word-pattern analysis of the languages of psychopaths. *Legal and Criminological Psychology, 18*, 102–114.

Hardalov, M., Koychev, I., & Nakov, P. (2016). In search of credible news. In: *Artificial intelligence: Methodology, systems, and applications. 17th International conference*, AIMSA, Varna, Bulgaria.

Herman, E. (2017). Fake news on Russia and other official enemies. *The New York Times, 1917–2017*. Available from https://doi.org/10.14452/MR-069-03-2017-07_8. <https://monthlyreview.org/2017/07/01/fake-news-on-russia-and-other-official-enemies/>.

Holan, A.D. (2016). *2016 Lie of the year: Fake news*. Retrieved from <www.politifact.com/truth-o-meter/article/2016/dec/13/2016-lie-year-fake-news/>.

Homonoff, H. (2017). *Ken Burns' 'The Vietnam War' echoes journalists' battle against fake news*. Retrieved February 5, 2018 from <https://www.forbes.com/sites/howardhomonoff/2017/09/29/ken-burns-vietnam-war-echoes-of-journalists-battle-against-fake-news/#3fe1bb972a78>.

Lippmann, W., & Merz, C. (1920). *A test of the news*. New York: New Republic.

Manago, A. M., Graham, M. B., Greenfield, P. M., & Salimkhan, G. (2008). Self-presentation and gender on MySpace. *Journal of Applied Developmental Psychology, 29*(6), 446–458. Available from https://doi.org/10.1016/j.appdev.2008.07.001.

Memmott, M. (2013). *75 Years ago, war of the worlds started a panic. Or did it?* Retrieved February 10, 2018, from <https://www.npr.org/sections/thetwo-way/2013/10/30/241797346/75-years-ago-war-of-the-worlds-started-a-panic-or-did-it>.

Oh, O., Agrawal, M., & Rao, H. R. (2013). Community intelligence and social media services: a rumor theoretic analysis of tweets during social crises. *MIS Quarterly, 37*(2), 407–426.

Peterson, H. (2013). 'Catfishing:' The phenomenon of Internet scammers who fabricate online identities and entire social circles to trick people into romantic relationships. Retrieved from https://www.dailymail.co.uk/news/article-2264053/Catfishing-The-phenomenon-Internet-scammers-fabricate-online-identities-entire-social-circles-trick-people-romantic-relationships.html.

Pressman, G. (2012). *Remembering the Great Moon Hoax of 1835*. Retrieved February 9, 2018, from <https://www.nbcnewyork.com/news/local/moon-hoax-166810096.html>.

Rheingold, H. (1993). *The virtual community: Homesteading on the electronic frontier*. Reading, MA: Addison-Wesley.

Rubin, V. L., & Lukoianova, T. (2015). Truth and deception at the rhetorical structure level. *Journal of the Association for Information Science and Technology, 66*, 905–917.

Schwartz, A. B. (2015). *The infamous "war of the worlds" radio broadcast was a magnificent fluke*. Retrieved February 10, 2018, from <https://www.smithsonianmag.com/history/infamous-war-worlds-radio-broadcast-was-magnificent-fluke-180955180>.

Serota, K. B., Levine, T. R., & Boster, F. J. (2010). The Prevalence of lying in America: Three studies of self-reported lies. *Human Communication Research, 36*(1), 2–25. Available from https://doi.org/10.1111/j.1468-2958.2009.01366.x.

Silverman, C. (2016). This analysis shows how fake election news stories outperformed real news on Facebook. *BuzzFeed News*, November 16.

Silverman, C., & Singer-Vine, J. (2016). Most Americans who see fake news believe it, new survey says. *BuzzFeed News*, December 6.

Spector, R. H. (2018). *Vietnam War 1954–1975*. Retrieved February 5, 2018, from <https://www.britannica.com/event/Vietnam-War>.

Starbird, K., Maddock, J., Orand, M., Achterman, P., & Mason, R. M. (2014). Rumors, false flags, and digital vigilantes: Misinformation on Twitter after the 2013 Boston marathon bombing. In: *iConference 2014 proceedings* (pp. 654–662). <https://doi.org/10.9776/14308>.

Toma, C. L., Hancock, J. T., & Ellison, N. B. (2008). Separating fact from fiction: an examination of deceptive self-presentation in online dating profiles. *Personality & Social Psychology Bulletin, 34*(8), 1023–1036.

Tsikerdekis, M., & Zeadally, S. (2014). Online deception in social media. *Communications of the ACM, 57*(9), 72–80. Available from https://doi.org/10.1145/2629612.

Vishwanath, A. (2014). Habitual Facebook use and its impact on getting deceived on social media. *Journal of Computer-Mediated Communication, 20*(1), 83–98.

Walther, J. B. (2007). Selective self-presentation in computer-mediated communication: Hyperpersonal dimensions of technology language, and cognition. *Computers in Human Behavior, 23*, 2538–2557. Available from https://doi.org/10.1016/j.chb.2006.05.002.

Wemple, E. (2013). *Fox News gaffe helps Muslim cultural museum*. Retrieved February 05, 2018, from <https://www.washingtonpost.com/blogs/erik-wemple/wp/2013/10/14/fox-news-gaffe-helps-muslim-cultural-museum/?utm_term = .597500d246a6>.

Whitty, M. T. (2002). Liar, liar! An examination of how open, supportive and honest people are in chat rooms. *Computers in Human Behavior, 18*, 343–352. Available from https://doi.org/10.1016/S0747-5632(01)00059-0.

Whitty, M. T., Buchanan, T., Joinson, A. N., & Meredith, A. (2012). Not all lies are spontaneous: An examination of deception across different modes of communication. *Journal of the American Society for Information Science & Technology, 63*(1), 208. Available from https://doi.org/10.1002/asi.21648.

Wright, D. E. (1999). *Personal relationships: An interdisciplinary approach*. Mountain View, CA: Mayfield Publishing Press.

Zahavi, A. (1993). The fallacy of conventional signaling. *Philosophical Transactions of the Royal Society of London, 340*, 227–230.

Zhao, L., Yin, J., & Song, Y. (2016). An exploration of rumor combating behavior on social media in the context of social crises. *Computers in Human Behavior, 58*, 25–36.

Zielinski, S. (2015). *The Great Moon Hoax was simply a sign of its time*. Retrieved February 09, 2018, from <https://www.smithsonianmag.com/smithsonian-institution/great-moon-hoax-was-simply-sign-its-time-180955761/>.

Zubiaga, A., Liakata, M., Procter, R., Hoi, G. W., & Tolmie, P. (2016). Analyzing how people orient to and spread rumors in social media by looking at conversational threads. *PLoS One, 11*(3).

III. THE DARK SIDE OF SOCIAL MEDIA USE FOR SOCIETIES

Index

Online (*Continued*)
  deception and deception using social
    media, 152–154
  ethnography, 93
  privacy literacy, 144
Online firestorms, 119
  CBAs, 119–126
  and dark side of social media, 128–129
  social media marketing, 119
  Union Street Guest House, 127–128
Openness, 33–34
ORI. *See* Obsessive relational intrusion
  (ORI)

P
Pacer Portal, 54
Pathological Internet use (PIU), 11
Patriotic vegetarians, 128–129
Personal
  autonomy, 137
  identity, 145
  relationships, 145
Personality, 53–54
Phone apps to deal with bullying,
  53–54
Physical attraction, 27–28
(Pin)boards, 62
Pinball
  machine, 117–118
  metaphor, 122
Pinterest, 66–69
PIU. *See* Pathological Internet use (PIU)
Political disagreements, 84–85
Politics, 84
Positive tonality, 106
Postbreakup, 82–83
Pragmatists, 139–140
Premediated cyberbullying, 50–51
Presentation of Self in Everyday Life, The
  (Goffman), 154
Pretesting of content, 129t
Primary narcissism, 24
Primordial personality traits, 33–34
Privacy, 137–138
  control, 138
  literacy, 144–145
  paradox, 139–144
  rules, 138
  on social media, 145–146
  turbulence, 138
Problematic overuse of social media.
  See Social media addiction

Psychological abuse, 49
Psychopaths, 29–30
Psychopathy, 34–35

R
Random agreement probability, 101
RDT. *See* Relational dialectics theory (RDT)
Real Instagram accounts (RINSTAs),
  52–53, 53t
Relational dialectics theory (RDT), 77–78
Relationship dissolution model, 81–82
Relationship drama, social media and
  problems in friendship relationships,
    83–85
  romantic relationship problems, 75–83
Representativity, lack of, 102–105
Responsibilities and competencies, 129t
RINSTAs. *See* Real Instagram accounts
  (RINSTAs)
Romantic jealousy, 75–76
Romantic relationship problems
  abuse and violence, 80
  dialectic tensions, 77–78
  infidelity, 78–80
  jealousy, 75–77
  postbreakup, 82–83
  relationship dissolution, 81–82
Rumination, 6
Rumors, 156–158
Russian Bolshevik revolution, 160

S
Scamming, 153–154
Secondary narcissism, 24
Self-determination theory (SDT), 10
Self-esteem, 62
Self-evaluation, 137
Self-presentation lies, 154–156
Self-selection bias, 103
Selfie-editing, 67–68
Selfies, 13, 32
Selfitis, 13
Sender deception, 152
Sentiment, 108
Serotonin, 12
Sex differences in cyberbullying, 49–50
Sexual activity online, 144–145
Sexual communication websites, 153
Sharenting, 143
Shitstorm, 119
Skepticism, 156–157

Printed in the United States
By Bookmasters